CONCILIUM

Religion in the Eighties

CONCILIUM

Concilium 188 (6/1986): Special Issue

SYNOD 1985 –
AN EVALUATION

Edited by
Giuseppe Alberigo
and
James Provost

English Language Editor
Marcus Lefébure

T. & T. CLARK LTD
Edinburgh

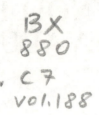

December 1986
T & T Clark Ltd, 59 George Street, Edinburgh EH2 2LQ
ISBN: 0 567 30068 4

ISSN: 0010-5236

Typeset by Print Origination Formby Liverpool
Printed by Page Brothers (Norwich) Ltd

Concilium: Published February, April, June, August, October, December.
Subscriptions 1986: UK: £19.95 (including postage and packing); USA: US$40.00
(including air mail postage and packing): Canada: Canadian $50.00 (including air
mail postage and packing); other countries: £19.95 (including postage and packing).

CONTENTS

Part I
The Preparation

Part II
The Meeting

Part III
The Consequences of the Synod

ANNOUNCEMENT

Starting with the first issue of 1987, there will be a special article or 'column' in each issue of *Concilium* on a topic of current interest. These articles will not necessarily be related to the themes of the issues in which they appear, but will be prepared immediately before each issue goes to press to provide immediate comment on current affairs.

EDITORIAL

THE EVENT of the 1985 Extraordinary Synod of Bishops occasioned considerable publicity and discussion prior to the event. The editors of *Concilium* themselves issued a statement as part of this general attention toward the Synod. During the two weeks of the Synod meeting itself the presence of the world press gave witness to the interest and expectations which this event engendered.

Within days or weeks, however, the Synod seemed to disappear from public consciousness. What had been anticipated as being so noteworthy became almost a 'non-event' to the popular and religious press.

The reality of this Extraordinary Synod, however, is only now beginning to be appreciated. Called to evaluate the results of Vatican II after twenty years of experience, the Synod in many ways presents us with an unexpectedly fruitful witness of a Church in the process of being transformed, a valuable balance sheet of a reform in progress.

As with any process, the one to which the synod bears witness is complex. In this volume we present an evaluation of the Synod which does not shrink from addressing this complexity, without pretending to be an exhaustive analysis or comprehensive synthesis. Rather, our authors have attempted to highlight key elements in the reality of the Synod—and in the life of the Church to which the Synod testifies—as a means of stimulating a greater appreciation for the complex mystery of God's people on the road, of this pilgrim people realising its mission in ever changing times and multiple cultures.

Our evaluation moves through three stages: the preparation for the Synod, the meeting itself, and the consequence of the Synod with special attention to issues identified in the Synod's Final Report. Although working independently, our authors have verified several common elements throughout these three stages, confirming the vitality of the Catholic Church as it implements Vatican II but also the complexity of a Church with many different tendencies in diverse cultures.

In a *first stage* four studies explore the situation of the Church as the Synod opened. A. Dulles surveys the concerns of theologians, particularly in ecclesiology as it emerges in the works which have appeared in the twenty years since Vatican II. A. Melloni, on the other hand, explores the reality of the Church at this distance from Vatican II, as it is perceived by bishops and expressed in the presynodal reports filed by a number of bishops' conferences. These two studies produce complementary pictures of issues remaining to be solved and of experiences which witness to the dynamism of Vatican II.

Two other studies explore specific documents presented immediately prior to the Synod which witness to the tensions in the postconciliar Church. J. Provost explores the proposed reform of the Roman Curia. R. Muñoz comments on the document issued by the International Theological Commission in view of the Synod meeting.

Four papers examine the *Synodal meeting itself* J. Kerkofs presents a statistical analysis of the participants and the Synod and compares the results with participants at Vatican II and at other Synod assemblies. A revealing portrait of the postconciliar Church emerges, a Church becoming in K. Rahner's terms a 'world Church'.

J. Komonchak illustrates the various stages of the Synodal debates by following the development of key ecclesiological issues, from the preliminary report at the opening of the Synod to the Final Report issued by the Synod. This final document is itself analysed by J-M. Tillard, who finds it to be a reception yet also a rereading of Vatican II by the Bishops of the Synod, many of whom were not at Vatican II. From this point of view Cardinal Lorscheider's witness is particularly interesting.

The *final portion* of the volume addresses various issues which the Synod identified as requiring further study. The authors have placed these issues in their conciliar and postconciliar contexts in an effort to situate the Synod's proposals in a correct perspective.

The proposal to develop a 'catechism or compendium of all Catholic doctrine' is viewed by a bishop and by a scholar. Bishop E. Zoghby calls for greater sensitivity to cultural diversity and the evangelical dimension of catechesis, and argues against the imposition of a catechism which is written in a limited perspective. B. Marthaler demonstrates through the history of proposals at Vatican I, Vatican II and various assemblies of the Synod of Bishops, that the proposed compendium is not a children's catechism. Rather, it must be seen in the same direction as the General Catechetical Directory mandated by Vatican II.

H. Pottmeyer places the discussion of Church as mystery, as communion, and as institution, in the context of Vatican II, postconciliar theological discussion, and the Final Report of the Synod. H. Teissier sets the agenda for a study of the theological status of conferences of bishops, drawing on patristic sources as well as the teaching of Vatican II.

The role of *subsidiarity* in the Church, after being favourably adopted in the revision of the Code of Canon Law, was questioned in the Synod's Final Report. P. Huizing explores the significance of this question. The Synod also called for an 'option for the poor'. The pastoral implications of such a position are witnessed by J. Gaillot from his personal experiences as a bishop. Several issues addressed in the Synod's Final Report reflect an identifiable view of the relation of Church and world, itself one of the significant topics at Vatican II. G. Ruggieri examines several elements in the Final Report to pose the critical options which must be faced in the light of the Synod.

A more long-term consequence of the 1985 Extraordinary Synod, one which may remain long after the above issues have been superseded, is the *new sense of being Church* which was almost taken for granted and which found living expression in the Synod. G. Alberigo demonstrates how, despite the unusual elements which marked the preparation and celebration of the Synod, an awareness of Church and its mission emerged. This awareness is truly influenced by Vatican II, and is evident in the various presynodal reports of conferences of bishops and even in the final Synod document itself.

The event of the 1985 Extraordinary Synod is now an historical fact, to be appreciated in its proper context with its elements of insight and of compromise, of faith and ecclesial politics, as with any other Church gathering of our time. But the reality of the Synod is, on balance, a continued witness to the pilgrimage of God's people enlightened by John XXIII's 'new Pentecost' and, under God's Word, making present in diverse cultures the continuing presence of Christ in our times.

Giuseppe Alberigo
James H. Provost

PART I

The Preparation

Avery Dulles

Catholic Ecclesiology Since Vatican II

ANY OVERVIEW of Catholic ecclesiology in the past twenty years must centre on Vatican II, which established nearly all the main themes. The ideas that surfaced at the Council, to be sure, were not produced out of nothing. Practically all these ideas had been discussed at some depth in the theological literature of the preceding decades, especially in the circle of theologians in contact with Yves Congar. Without this *previous theological reflection* on episcopacy, collegiality, ecumenism, Church reform, the role of the laity, religious freedom, and liturgical renewal—to mention only a few themes that come to mind—the achievements of Vatican II would not have been possible. The Council, however, gave entirely new status to what had previously been mere speculation on the part of *avantgarde*, and in some cases suspect, theologians. Through conciliar endorsement many of these ideas became *established Catholic doctrine*. Vatican II, therefore, provided a new starting point, making it almost superfluous to refer to the preconciliar phase. The Council itself may therefore serve as the primary focus for the present article.

Wisely in my opinion, the Council did not commit itself to any particular theological school. It attempted to achieve and express a broad Catholic consensus and to leave open any questions that did not yet seem ripe for decision. In this respect Vatican II followed the practice of many previous Councils, including Constantinople, Ephesus, Chalcedon, and Trent. The well-known ambiguities of Vatican II are not shady compromises in the sense of trade-offs between rival parties but, for the most part, common decisions to protect the freedom of Catholics to probe more deeply into matters still requiring clarification.

1.   NATURE OF THE CHURCH

The most basic of these undecided questions has to do with the very nature of the Church itself. The Council deliberately refrained from attempting a definition in the Aristotelian sense. The first chapter of the Constitution on the Church presents the Church as an *aspect of the mystery of Christ*, thereby implying that the Church immeasurably transcends all human concepts and formulations. After considering various biblical metaphors such as flock, vineyard, temple, mother and spouse, the Constitution proceeds to discuss two images, Body of Christ and People of God, at greater length. The Church, moreover, is in several key passages described as 'sacrament of unity' (*LG* 1) or 'universal sacrament of salvation' (*LG* 48). The institutional aspects of the Church, so heavily emphasised in post-Tridentine Catholicism, are somewhat subordinated, inasmuch chapter III on the hierarchy was placed, in the final text, *after* chapter II on the people of God.

By operating with a variety of metaphors or paradigms, the Council may be said to have set the stage for the discussion of 'models' that has been prominent in the ecclesiology of the past twenty years.[1] The various models, without directly contradicting one another, *highlight different aspects and functions*, suggesting different priorities and goals. It remains to be seen whether the different themes of Vatican II can be integrated into an overall synthesis and articulated by means of a single overarching model. Following a suggestion of Pope John Paul II, I have proposed that the image of 'community of disciples' may be used to integrate the elements found in the preceding five models.[2] From a somewhat different perspective the Extraordinary Synod of 1985 attempted to synthesise the Church's apostolates of evangelisation, ecumenism, and social transformation in the light of an *ecclesiology of mystery and communion*. According to the Final Report, 'The church as communion is a sacrament for the salvation of the world.'[3]

2.   CHURCH, WORLD AND KINGDOM

The different perspectives on the Church affect the discussion of all the problem areas to which we now turn. For example, there is a variety of opinions about how the Church is related to the kingdom of God. Vatican II stated that the Church is 'the kingdom of God now present in mystery' (*LG* 3) and that the Church 'becomes on earth the initial budding forth of that kingdom' (*LG* 5). But if left open the questions whether the kingdom is present on earth beyond the borders of the Church and whether the final kingdom will be anything other than the Church itself in its final glorious condition.[4]

Ecclesiologists committed to the 'servant' model tend to see the Church as *one of many agencies intended to make the world a place of freedom, peace, justice, and prosperity*. These values, rather than specifically religious features, are seen as embodiments of the kingdom. But other theologians, who prefer to think of the Church as the Body of Christ or, in a strongly realistic sense, the sacrament of Christ, hold that the *Church exists in a certain sense for its own sake*. For them, the Church alone is the embodiment on earth of the kingdom of God. A tension between these two perspectives on the Church-kingdom relationship pervades much of the post-conciliar Catholic literature on ecclesiology.

Much of the energy of ecclesiologists since Vatican II has been taken up in the attempt to clarify the relationship between the *Church and the world*, which entered into a new phase with the Council's Pastoral Constitution on the Church in the Modern World. Catholics have rightly felt a certain corporate responsibility for the *defence of human life and the promotion of human rights*. But as they have sought to give concrete expression to these concerns they have found themselves divided against fellow Christians and fellow Catholics. Grave problems have arisen with respect to the official involvement of the Church in social and political issues. The recent tendency seems to be to insist that the defence of human rights against oppressive systems of government pertains integrally to the preaching of the Gospel, but to maintain at the same time that the official Church, including its bishops and priests, should abstain from partisan politics. The distinction is a very fine one and has led to some misunderstandings within the Church. But it is imperative for the Church on the one hand to avoid a retreat into the sacristy and on the other, to keep from becoming excessively entangled in the struggles of practical politics.

3. ECUMENISM AND MISSION

Vatican II firmly committed the Catholic Church to ecumenism but refrained from deciding in advance the subtler questions proposed as subjects for dialogue. Thus the Council spoke vaguely about the ecclesial status of non-Roman Catholic Christians and about the sacraments and ministries of Anglican and Protestant churches. Disputes continue to rage about the correct interpretation of the statement that the *Church of Christ 'subsists in'* *the Roman Catholic Church* (*LG* 8). Many theologians, pointing out that this term was introduced to replace 'is' in the previous draft, argue that the Council in effect repudiated the Pius XII's doctrine that the Mystical Body is exclusively identical with the Roman Catholic communion. A few theologians make the further inference that the Catholic Church, being only a part of the Church of Christ, may not properly act as if it were the whole. They then go on to call into question the ecumenicity of councils at which only Roman Catholics have a deliberative voice, and the validity of dogmas defined by the authority of Roman Catholic councils or popes. More conservative theologians contend that the term 'subsists' was chosen precisely to indicate that the totality of the Church of Christ is present in Catholicism, and hence that other Christians are, at least to some degree, separated from the true Church.

Vatican II, in fact, proposed a nuanced position that makes it inadequate to regard the Catholic Church *either as the whole or as a mere part of the Church of Christ*. The Church of Christ is verified in Roman Catholicism in its institutional fullness, but because ecclesial elements such as the Scriptures, sacraments, and various forms of prayer and worship are to be found beyond the official borders of Roman Catholicism, one may say that the Church of Christ is present in various degrees and modalities in other Christian communities.[5] Thanks to the ecclesial elements in these communities, their members can enjoy a true communion with Christ and stand in a certain, though incomplete, communion with the Catholic Church. The ecumenical apostolate aims to prepare the way for full reconciliation and communion among the churches.

The enthusiasm tended to *overshadow the traditional forms of missionary activity*. The post-conciliar years have proved to be a difficult period for missionary work. The teaching of the Council regarding the positive values of the non-Christian religions and the possibilities of salvation for the unevangelised destroyed what had been for many the prime motive for missionary work. Theologians such as Rahner attempted to construct a rationale for missions compatible with a highly optimistic view of the religious situation of 'anonymous Christians', but this rationale was too subtle and complex to gain a wide following. Some clarity was at length brought to the situation by the apostolic exhortation, *Evangelii nuntiandi*, issued by Paul VI in 1975. Since that time the idea of evangelisation has begun to gain ground in Catholic circles, but a convincing up-to-date missiology still remains to be constructed.

4. UNITY AND INNER DIVERSITY

Another theme which the Council opened up for further exploration is that of the *inner diversity within the Catholic Church itself*. For the first time in history, the Catholic Church appeared at Vatican II as firmly implanted in every continent. The Council documents drew the conclusion that each major sociocultural area ought to develop *forms of theology and religious life suitable to itself*, yet free from all syncretism and false particularism (*AG* 22). Thus the Church should foster and take to herself the resources and customs of each people (*LG* 13). Rome, as the touchstone of unity, was assigned a double function: to protect legitimate differences and to see that those differences do not hinder unity but rather contribute to it (*LG* 13). These and similar directives were taken by many as an encouragement for enculturation. Very quickly, however, problems arose as to *the limits of this process*. To what extent should regional churches be encouraged to devise their own liturgical forms and their own formulations of doctrine? Are all cultures equally hospitable to authentic Christianity or do the cultures, as Paul VI taught in *Evangelii nuntiandi* (*EN* 20), need to be 'evangelised'? How can such an evangelisation of cultures be distinguished from the intrusion of foreign cultures, from spiritual colonisation? Both Paul VI and John Paul II have frequently grappled with these questions, providing a body of documentation that goes far beyond the brief indications given by Vatican II. Some authors now speak of a 'wonderful exchange': the gospel discloses and liberates the true and abiding values in every culture, whereas the cultures, by giving original expressions to the Gospel, manifest new aspects of the Gospel.[6]

Still another point left undecided by the Council was the *relative priority of the universal and the local Church*. In other words: does the local church come about through an inner differentiation of the universal Church, or does the universal Church, on the contrary, arise through the conjunction of local churches? Different passages from the Council documents can be cited in favour of one or the other of these positions (e.g., *LG* 26; *CD* 11). It makes some difference whether the Church of Christ is seen to be fully, or only partially, present in the local church (which may, in turn, be seen as the regional church, the diocese, the parish, or a smaller eucharistic assembly). Divisions of opinion on this matter seem to lurk behind the existing disagreements as to whether the *principle of subsidiarity* applies to the Church—a problem taken up in another article in the present volume. The principle of subsidiarity is more obviously applicable if the universal Church is simply a gathering of local churches, each possessing in itself all the essentials of the Church.

5. PRIMACY AND COLLEGIALITY

Numerous questions regarding the internal organisation of the Church were left open by Vatican II. Most fundamental perhaps was the set of problems surrounding the *principle of collegiality*. The principle itself was resoundingly endorsed by the Council, but no precise interpretation was imposed. Since the council *two contrary opinions have competed for accept-*

ance.[7] Theologians of the first school hold that there are two inadequately distinct subjects of supreme power in the Church—the pope and the college of bishops. The pope, as head of the college, can exercise his supreme power either personally or collegially, whereas other bishops can exercise it only collegially. This view of the matter seems to be favoured by the *nota praevia* of the Theological Commission, which is included in many editions of the Council documents. But a second view can also be defended as consistent with the teaching of Vatican II—namely that the supreme power in the Church is situated only in the college made up of the pope and his fellow bishops. Every exercise of this supreme power is collegial, for the pope never acts as pope except when he acts in union with, and as head of, the college. This latter view, which enjoys the support of Congar and Rahner, raises many further questions about the power of the pope to act without, or even against, the majority opinion of his fellow bishops. Can one meaningfully say that even when he reserves decisions to himself he is acting collegially?

The *status of the Roman curia and that of the synod of bishops are primarily canonical rather than theological questions.* It is worth noting, however, that theological issues are at stake in the discussions. Is the Roman curia an agency of the pope as bishop of Rome or should it be under the control and at the service of the worldwide episcopate? The efforts of Paul VI, in response to Vatican II, to internationalise the curia—and even his action in adding some residential bishops to the various Roman congregations—do not solve this theoretical question. Connected with it is the question whether the college of cardinals itself is a collegial body capable of making decisions in common, or simply a body of advisors to the pope, who never act decisively except in electing a new pope.

The *synod of bishops* was set up by Paul VI in *Apostolica sollicitudo* (September 15, 1965) in response to many requests at the council for an organ permanently expressing the collegiality of the bishops. But it is not clear from the pope's *motu proprio*, from the council documents, or from the revised Code of Canon Law whether this synod is a properly collegial institution or one that pertains rather to the pope in his exercise of the primacy. The fact that the majority of the members are elected by the episcopal conferences and are invited to represent their conferences suggests that the synod has a genuinely collegial character. But the fact that it acts only in an advisory capacity, and meets only at the summons of the pope, tells rather in favour of its service to the pope in his function as universal primate.

The statements of Vatican II regarding *regional and national episcopal conferences* were fraught with much tension and ambiguity. No decision was made as to whether such conferences are to be seen as implementing the principle of collegiality. In the strictest sense collegial actions are those which proceed from the universal episcopate as a united body. But many theologians, correctly in my opinion, look upon the conferences as limited expressions of collegiality, implementing what Vatican II referred to as the 'collegial spirit' (*affectus collegialis, LG* 23). The International Theological Commission, to the surprise of some theologians recently declared that episcopal conferences are not collegial except in 'an analogous, theologically improper sense.'[8] The Synod of 1985 has called for a deeper study of the theological status and doctrinal authority of episcopal conferences.

6. MAGISTERIUM AND DISSENT

Yet another problem that Vatican II bequeathed to the post-conciliar Church has to do with the relationship between the *ecclesiastical magisterium and theologians*. The Council said very little explicitly about the role and authority of theologians. The Pastoral Constitution on the Church in the Modern World encouraged theologians to seek continually for more suitable ways of communicating doctrine to their contemporaries (*GS* 62), and the Constitution on Divine Revelation paid tribute to the work of *biblical scholars* in helping to mature the judgment of the Church (*DV* 12). The Decree on Ecumenism conceded that there might be deficiencies in official formulations of doctrine—as distinguished from the deposit of faith itself (*UR* 6). The Constitution on the Church, however, insisted on the duty of all Catholics to submit to the *magisterium* of the pope and bishops, even when no claim is made to infallibility (*LG* 25). The Council's Theological Commission rejected several requests to deal with the problem of legitimate dissent.

Yet the actual practice of the Council ineluctably raised the question of dissent. On a number of well-known issues (e.g., historical-critical exegesis, ecumenism, and religious freedom) Vatican II vindicated theologians whose orthodoxy had been under suspicion a decade earlier. Thus reflective persons could not help but ask: Can there be such a thing as *loyal opposition in the Church*? Does the theologian sometimes have the right and duty to withhold assent from currently official teachings that are, in principle, reformable? Could not public advocacy of doctrinal change be an appropriate way of preparing for a desirable development of doctrine? If these questions are affirmatively answered, it must further be asked whether the *magisterium* would still be in a position to teach with binding authority, and, if not, whether the power of the Church itself to bear effective witness to the Gospel would not ultimately be eroded. These questions are not empty abstractions. They received a number of concrete applications in the decade following the Council, especially in connection with Paul VI's 'birth control' encyclical,

Humanae vitae (1968). This encyclical, rejected by the large majority of priests, theologians and laity in many parts of the world, became a kind of test case for one's views on the authority of the *magisterium*. The lack of agreed norms and procedures for dealing with cases of *conscientious dissent* is a major source of tension and malaise in the Church and the theological community.[9]

7. MINISTRIES

A final area in which much work remains to be done is the theology of *ministry*. Vatican II raised the order of bishops to unprecedented heights by emphasising their powers to teach, rule, and sanctify as successors of the apostles. Yet the Council sought not to degrade priests, deacons, and lay persons in the Church.

The Council is generally perceived as having demystified the priesthood by distancing itself from the highly sacralised theology of orders characteristic of medieval and post-Tridentine Catholicism. Broadly speaking, the approach to priesthood is pastoral and functional. The Constitution on the Church, however, clearly affirmed that the ordained priest acts at the altar 'in the person of Christ' and that his priesthood differs in essence, not simply in degree, from the common priesthood of the faithful (*LG* 10). These hierarchical features of the priesthood, reaffirmed by the synod of bishops in 1971, are difficult to harmonise with the more community-oriented theologies of ministry that have emerged since Vatican II in many parts of the world.

The Council further strengthened the hierarchy by authorising the restoration of the permanent diaconate in churches of the Latin rite (*LG* 29). But the precise functions of the permanent diaconate were left rather vague. In the past two decades there have been serious disagreements between some who see the primary role of the deacon as helping the priest in liturgical functions and others who see him as having a predominantly secular role in works of charity and justice. Many deplore the 'clericalisation' of the diaconate, seemingly on the ground that a kind of 'third race' is needed to build a bridge between a clericalised priesthood and a secularised laity.

Regarding the *laity*, the Council may be said to have endorsed the cautious but constructive proposals advanced by theologians such as Congar in the 1950s. Congar had given the laity a secure place in the 'life', but not in the 'structure', of the Church.[10] The Council, like Congar, designated the world, rather than the Church, as the primary sphere for the lay apostolate (*LG* 31). Within the Church, pastors were admonished to 'listen to the laity willingly' and, on suitable occasions, to invite them to use their own initiative (*PO* 9).

But neither the Council documents nor the revised Code of Canon Law gave any real power to the laity. As compared with many civil governments, the Church falls short in providing its members with effective means of vindicating their rights. In spite of some progress since the Council, the ministerial gifts of *women* are insufficiently utilised. The patriarchalism of traditional theology has not been fully overcome.

The *theologies of ministry* that have begun to blossom since the Council may be crucially important for the ecclesiology of the future. In these theologies the hierarchical stratification of the Church into classes is being offset, to some degree, by a *theology of interrelated gifts and callings*. Authority is perceived as depending *less on office and power* than on *charism and service*. Elements of this pneumatic and organic approach, scripturally grounded in Paul's First Letter to the Corinthians, may be discerned in chapter II of the Constitution on the Church.

8. HERMENEUTICS OF THE COUNCIL

In all the preceding problem areas one may discern *two general tendencies*. Liberal or progressive Catholics are inclined to interpret Vatican II in sharp contrast to the preceding period. For them the Council marked the end of post-Tridentine Catholicism and the dawn of a new era. Writers of this mentality frequently characterise the preceding centuries by pejorative terms such as dogmatism, juridicism, clericalism, and authoritarianism. They describe preconciliar Catholicism as static, defensive, polemical, sacral, hierarchical, monolithic, and centralist, in contrast to a new era which is seen as personalist, participatory, communal, dynamic, open, dialogic, and pluralistic. Progressive Catholics, in their turn, are viewed by more traditional thinkers as tainted with liberalism, secularism, laicism, and modernism, and as promoting unacceptable pluralism. In the decade following the Council Catholics became *polarised into two camps*, and great pressure was put on individuals to adopt the total party line of one camp or the other.

Even before the Council came to an end the progressives captured the initiative in interpreting the documents as supporting their own positions. Although they recognised that certain statements in the documents favoured their opponents, they tended to appeal from the letter to the spirit of Vatican II. The spirit they found in the dynamic interpretation. Some commentators proposed that *a proper hermeneutics* would find the key to the Council's meaning in its innovations. Wherever the Council simply repeated what had previously been taught, this was attributed to inertia, to perfunctory rhetoric, or to the necessity of placating the conservative minority. Conservative interpreters, by contrast, tended to use the Council's reaffirmations of the positions of Trent, Vatican I, and Pius XII as the hermeneutical key for understanding all other passages.

In the second decade after the Council these *one-sided interpretations have been vigorously challenged*. Theologians such as Walter Kasper and Hermann-Josef Pottmeyer have protested against selective interpretations that seek to perpetuate the very battles which the Council, through its consensus, overcame in principle. The spirit of Vatican II cannot be urged against the letter, nor can it be plausibly maintained that the majority of the bishops wished to break with the earlier Catholic tradition.[11] The Council's documents must therefore be understood *not selectively but integrally*, not in opposition to, but in continuity with, the Catholicism of earlier centuries. Where the Council was content simply to juxtapose traditional and innovative formulations, the interpreters are challenged to seek a *coherent synthesis that does justice to both*.[12]

The question before the Extraordinary Synod of 1985 was not—as some commentators imagined—whether to affirm or reject Vatican II, but rather *how to interpret it*. The Synod in its Final Report laid down some eminently sane *hermeneutical principles*. In the first place, one must pay attention to all the Council documents in their *interrelationship*, taking particular note of the four major Constitutions. Secondly, one must avoid playing off the pastoral character of the Council against its doctrinal import or opposing the letter of the Council to its spirit. Thirdly, Vatican II must be understood in continuity with the great tradition of the Church. And finally, we must allow the Council to enlighten us as we strive to read the signs of our own times.[13]

In the brief time at its disposal the Synod was not able to achieve a full and coherent synthesis transcending all the polarisations of the recent past. But it did to some extent *point the way*. Guided by a hermeneutics of unity, the ecclesiology of the future may be able to correct some of the imbalances of the past two decades. It seems evident that a *less political and a more distinctively theological vision of the Church* must be achieved. If the Church were to be reformed according to the spiritual principles of the Gospel, it would no longer be a scene of disedifying party struggles. Interiorly united by mutual trust and love, the Church might once again be the kind of sign that it was to the pagans of ancient Greece and Rome. Dialogue and participation would no longer be seen as threats to authority and order, nor would office be seen as the enemy of freedom. Primacy and collegiality, hierarchy and laity, would be seen as mutually necessary and supportive. Ecclesiology cannot by itself bring about this kind of spiritual reformation, but it can at least show the urgency of some such renewal. For the Church to be truly itself it must be in manifest actuality a *structured community of disciples animated and unified by the Spirit of the risen Christ*.

Notes

1. A. Dulles *Models of the Church* (Garden City, N.Y. 1974). For another typology based on recent ecclesiological literature, see B. Mondin *Le nuove ecclesiologie* (Rome 1980).

2. A. Dulles *A Church to Believe In* (New York, N.Y. 1982). See John Paul II's Encyclical *Redemptor hominis* (1979) no. 21.

3. Synod of Bishops, The Final Report, II D 1; *Origins* 15:27 (19 Dec. 1985) 499.

4. The recent Report of the International Theological Commission, *The One Church of Christ*, states: 'It is evident that, in the teaching of the Council, there can be no difference, as to the reality to come about at the end of time, between the perfected Church (*consummata*) and the perfected kingdom (*consummatum*)' (no. 10-2). The Report also declares with regard to the terrestrial Church: 'To belong to the kingdom cannot fail to constitute a belonging—at least implicit—to the Church' (*ibid.*). See *L'unique Eglise du Christ* ed. P. Eyt (Paris 1985) pp. 68 and 70.

5. G. Baum 'The Ecclesial Reality of Other Churches' *Concilium* 4, *The Church and Ecumenism* (New York, N.Y. 1965) 62–86.

6. *L'unique Eglise du Christ*, cited in note 4, no. 4-2, p. 29.

7. These opinions are lucidly set forth in Y. Congar *Ministères et communion ecclésiale* (Paris 1971) pp. 187–227.

8. *L'unique Eglise du Christ*, cited in note 4, no. 5-3, p. 38.

9. See the Committee Report of the Canon Law Society of America and the Catholic Theological Society of America, *Cooperation between Theologians and the Ecclesiastical Magisterium* (Washington, D.C. 1982).

10. Y. Congar *Lay People in the Church* (Westminster, Md. 1957, ²1965) (*Jalons pour une théologie du laïcat*, Paris 1953, ³1964).

11. H.-J. Pottmeyer 'Vers une nouvelle phase de réception de Vatican II' in *La Réception de Vatican II* (Paris 1985) pp. 43–64, esp. pp. 56–58.

12. W. Kasper *Gesichtspunkte für die ausserordentliche Bischofssynode 1985*, typescript, 1–2.

13. Synod of Bishops, The Final Report, I, 5; *Origins* p. 445-46.

Alberto Melloni

After the Council and the Episcopal Conferences: the Responses

1. PREPARATORY CONSULTATION OF THE BISHOPS

HOWEVER WE judge the results of the Extraordinary Synod, it's clear that it was a *profound experience for the Church*. One way in which interest in the Synod and reflection on the Council was expressed was through the *consultation of bishops* instigated by the general secretariat elected by the previous ordinary synod.[1] This was done by sending patriarchs and presidents of episcopal conferences a questionnaire[2] and a programme of working rules (which included an introductory report, general discussion, discussion groups, reports from groups, conclusions). The views requested from the bishops' conferences and patriarchs were intended to serve as material for the initial report.

The bishops were given Vatican II as their ecclesiological 'ratio et cardo' and asked to examine the state of the Church with reference to the Council's insights on the Church 'ad intra et ad extra'. They were expressly asked four general and thirteen particular questions. The general questions asked what had been done to promote knowledge and acceptance of the Council among the faithful and to put its teaching into practice. What benefits had it brought in various regions? Had there been mistakes and abuses in the interpretation and application of the Council and what had been done to correct them? What difficulties had there been in accepting the new requirements for new times and what should the Synod do to develop Christian life in accordance with the spirit and letter of the Council. The particular questions amounted to a full-

14

scale questionnaire on the reception of individual documents, whose key themes were stated, often with brutal reductions.[3]

Although they only had six months, at the opening of the Council, the general secretariat had received 95 replies out of a possible 136.[4] This offered abundant material for the work of G. Daneels and W. Kasper whom the pope had appointed reporter and special secretary to the Synod respectively. The *value of these replies*, which have still been published only in part,[5] appears to me to be *twofold*. On the one hand, like the consultation eight years after the Council of Chalcedon in 451[6] the replies enable us to check on the reception given to an ecumenical assize in the opinion of the bishops. This is very necessary in the case of Vatican II, whose effects cannot be accounted for merely by statistics. On the other hand, in the still green experience of the Synod, consultation with the bishops in the absence of preparatory working documents has shown the high level of non-bureaucratic but specifically episcopal awareness of the bishops' conferences.

2. SIMILARITIES AND DISSIMILARITIES IN THE RESPONSES OF THE BISHOPS

I shall try to *present some of the themes and particular problems* dealt with by some of these replies, made accessible at the time of the Synod, from the 'report' which was intended to recapitulate them. I shall also draw from the speeches made in the chamber in which some of the conference chairmen summarised their documents.[7] There is substantial agreement in the material examined here, although there are some striking differences. This agreement could be the result of the accidental availability of publications by communally-minded bishops. But this does not seem probable. Moreover these documents have their own individual style. There are documents arising from broad consultation with the conference and others from work groups set up by the president as 'responses' which had to take the form of polemic or agreement with the questions asked by the secretary general. As many of these particular questions contained the presupposition that the Synod would demonstrate the limits of the reception of Vatican II, the replies had to deal with this problem. In general the conferences (as the final report confirms) were aware that they were expected to give more than a mere indication of the life of the Church in relation both to the topic addressed and to their particular circumstances. In fact the debate surrounding the preparation for the synod was dominated by certain topics and views, on which the churches were therefore obliged to take up a position.[8]

Of course one of the protagonists during this period was *J. Ratzinger*, who particularly through his *Report on the faith* had tried to suggest certain lines of interpretation for the post-conciliar era. This text is so well known that I do not need to summarise or discuss it. During the preparation for the Synod it was the subject of very heated debate, as the bishops were aware. Ratzinger's thesis, which received little agreement,[9] was that the last twenty years had been a time of disappointment and disorder for the Church, a time of 'crisis' and 'progressive decadence'. Other theologians criticised his approach on three counts. Some only touched lightly on the problem of the Council and maintained that Ratzinger's pessismism was because he was ill-informed, stuck within his limited Bavarian horizons in a sort of theological provincialism; according to these theologians the cardinal's analyses would be untenable outside Western Europe.[10] Others made judgment of the Council the keypoint of Ratzinger's analyses and replied that his report on the faith reversed causes and effects. In other words, it was the Council's cautiousness and limitations which explained the 'crisis' of Catholicism.[11] Yet a third group listed the individual provocations in Ratzinger's stated views (on bishops' conferences, liberation theology, africanisation, feminism etc), and pointed out the interdependence of these topics and their relevance to the question of how the Council should be accepted.[12]

3. THE VARIOUS WAYS IN WHICH THE BISHOPS DISTANCED THEMSELVES FROM THE NEGATIVE APPROACH

The conferences' responses were produced in this atmosphere. They confirm the impression that, beyond the particular criticisms directed at Ratzinger, he at least had the objective merit of *starting a debate which he was then unable to direct*. In the wake of the Anglo-Welsh conference, which was the first to produce its own document, the bishops did their best to grasp and communicate their own particular reality. The experience of making the inquiry was shared by all the conferences and profoundly affected their awareness. This showed in the paragraphs on communion in the final report. The conferences proved themselves and discovered themselves to be capable of transcending the limits that any individual one might unwarily have set in matters of theology or canon law. Their documents give us an irreplaceable and detailed *account of how the Council was received*.[13]

Nearly all the responses on which I have been able to work *distance themselves from the negative tone of part of the questionnaire of the secretary general and also from J. Ratzinger's hypotheses*. Some conferences, such as the Brazilian, answered the questions in a different order from that in which they were asked. Many others replied while ignoring the structure of the questionnaire. Others expressed unequivocal dissent. What I think is more interesting is to see how this differentiation took effect and to report certain passages. The replies and statements I saw had at least *four kinds of approach.*

(a) Some of the replies *distanced themselves from the negative anti-conciliar preconceptions* in an elliptical and cautious way by stressing the favourable acceptance of the Council in their churches. For example the *Anglo-Welsh* reply states that the Council's decrees 'have in general been welcomed'; the *Dutch* reply, dramatically charged with unresolved tensions, recognises 'positive data about the reception of the spirit and decisions' of the Council. The *Swiss* conference (which agrees with J. Ratzinger that the disinction between pre- and post-Council is 'a schematic view') recognises that 'during the last twenty years the Council has saved the Church from serious damage both in the manifestations of its inner life and in its attempts to be present to the world'. In the speech given in the hall in the name of his colleagues, the president of the *Caribbean* conference, held that 'the implementation of the decision of Vatican II has, in general, been exemplary and enormously beneficial to the churches of our region.' The *Syro-Malabar* church stated that 'during the period of the last twenty years a sincere effort has been made to make known to the faithful the teachings of Vatican II and to implement its directives'.

(b) A different method was used by those conferences which *faced the thesis of 'the Council as source of the crisis' head on and openly criticised it.* The most explicit in this sense was the *Italian* bishops' conference, which found the conviction that the Council was in itself—and continues in its good effects to be—an extraordinary grace from the Lord to be 'general and unquestioned. It cannot be said that all the difficulties whatever besetting the Church are the effect of the Council, or the way in which it was conducted or the trends proceeding from it'. The *French* conference held that the Council was 'our Church's great chance to come to terms with modern times' and that those who understand the Council as 'a message of faith and humanism' must welcome it 'in a genuine spirit of contemplation'. It added that 'it is unthinkable that any abuses in the application of the Council's guidelines should be taken as the cause of the Church's present difficulties'. The *Canadian* conference testified that the Council 'was well received on Canadian soil. It provoked neither significant division nor systematic rejection' and also stressed that 'it is important not to render Vatican II solely responsible for these numerous difficulties which have their roots elsewhere'. The *Gabon* bishops, who had local Lefebvrianism to deal with, reacted by stressing that 'those who criticise the conciliar reforms are often those whose Christian witness is the weakest'.

(c) Other conferences expressed their *support of the Council in purely positive terms.* For example the *US* conference began its own reply as follows:

'The Second Vatican Council was an authentic manifestation of the Holy Spirit at work in the Church'. Likewise the *Swedish* conference 'held at the time and still does today that the Second Vatican Council was very positive'. The *German* conference, rather more elliptically, also speaks of 'positive developments'. In his speech in the chamber the president of the *Togo* conference said: 'Vatican II . . . remains the event of the century' and that 'thus it was providential and Africa will always remember with gratitude that it was all through this celebration of the Church in Council that our autochthonous hierarchy was set up almost before our eyes'. The president of the *Thailand* conference declared that 'Vatican II starts a new era for the Church' which has brought a 'newness . . . visible in many areas'.

(d) A group of conferences, particularly from the *Third World, rejected the negative preconceptions about the Council*, but without adopting a position on the Council as such. They preferred to stress the positive nature of its results. The most forthright along these lines were the bishops from the countries of the *Mahgreb*, who declared 'on this twentieth anniversary, for us it is not a question of correcting errors but of giving new energy in the lives of our communities to the Council's great insights' (p.4). They added that 'although in our region the Council has not checked the growth of religious indifference for the great majority of the baptised, it has nevertheless given valuable things for the renewal of communities of practising Christians and especially for their leaders' (p.6). More briefly the *Zambia* conference declared that 'the Council has brought many good things to the life of the Church in our country' (p.1). The *Chad* conference stated that 'for a long time permanent education has been based on the documents of Vatican II'. In the first six pages of the 79 which comprise their voluminous document (which gathers the opinions of regional conferences and commissions), the *Brazilian* bishops list the positive fruits resulting from the Council (although they do not offer global judgments on the Council). They describe the Brazilian Church as 'very dynamic . . . more open, pilgrim and servant . . . prophetic . . . more decentralised and more articulated, more modern and with more participation', a church in which there is 'freedom, optimism, dialogue, initiative, creativity . . . a preferential option for the poor . . . widespread reform and transformation' (p.2). Then they consider these fruits in relation to the Church institutions, ministers, laity, the religious life, missionary aspects, the preaching of the Gospel, catechesis and theology, pastoral renewal, the liturgy and the spiritual life, ecumenism, the relations between the Church and the world and the promoting of a just and fraternal society. The president of the *Benin* conference also spoke in the chamber. He was very generous to the text of the international theological commission but also asked about the results of the Council: 'how would the Church face these situations today, if there had

never been a Vatican II?' The president of the *Bangladeshi* conference emphasised that the Council 'has brought about a true renewal of Christian life in our
Asian churches' and then went on to list the major points. Likewise the
bishops of *Belgium*, who made the point that Vatican II had ended the stage of
christendom, declared that 'the energy given to the life of the Church is thus
undeniable. And even though it has flagged over the years it is far from
exhausted.'

The general tone was only contradicted by the *Korean* conference document. Unlike all those quoted so far, this text gives a catastrophic picture in
reply to the question on the mistakes of the post-conciliar period. 'Interest in
horizontal human relations has come to supersede interest in vertical relationship with God. There is a tendency to ignore canon law in practice. Erroneous
interpretations of some points of dogma (. . .) have appeared, and a subjec-
tive, humanistic interpretation of ethical questions (. . .) has appeared; also
some priests have been extreme in their way of performing liturgy and
sacraments.'

This was the basis for their proposal—which had already been made in the
US bishops' document (although with very different emphasis)—which was
mentioned in the opening *relatio* and finally accepted by the pope at the
conclusion of the Synod: 'We recommend that the Vatican promulgate a
standard catechism text (Catechismus Romanus iuxta mentem Concilii
Vaticani II) in order to correct misunderstanding and lessen confusion.'[14]

These remarks by the bishops' conferences suggest a few comments. It
appears that the various churches related to the Council in an original and
dynamic way, showing that they had accepted to a far greater extent than was
foreseen the 'call to exist' made by Vatican II to the local churches. It is also
clear that for the most part the churches were unaffected by the pessimistic
suggestions authoritatively made by the secretary general, or even, through
worrying procedural mistakes, by the prefect of the congregation for the
teaching of the faith.

4. GETTING BEHIND THE GENERAL SIMILARITY OF RESPONSE

However these comments would be premature. Indeed we could think that
the general similarity in tone of the replies was not due to a true communion
but to external obedience to a Council behind which lay diverse opinions. We
can test this suspicion by reviewing a few more particular points of view and
the diagnosis of post-conciliar mistakes. We could point to the insistence of
some of the replies on the theme of subsidiarity (barely mentioned in Daneels'
report) and on that of bishops' conferences, which have become a cause of

tension. However these themes are of such wide relevance that they are among the keys to the whole Synod. Therefore I prefer here to dwell on *four less global but equally important aspects.*

(a) In reading the replies we realise that their almost *irreducible multiplicity* arises from the content of the choral witness borne to the Council. Indeed the more truly the churches have accepted the Council, the more this acceptance has been enriched by the relationship between Gospel and people.

(b) The temptation to transform the reception of the Council into the bureaucratic application of some *motu proprio* or liturgical book is shown up by the replies in all its fragility. These replies show how the acceptance of the Council developed with its own rhythm and energy, both in its more positive and more problematic aspects (admitted by all the epsicopal conferences). The key to judging liturgical and ecclesiological reform is how much the replies say about *scripture.* Where the Word was not dribbled out in little reforms which would have made change very gradual, it became the driving force for the Council's acceptance and the wheels on which it ran in every continent, from Europe to the Americas, Asia to Africa.

(c) There was a further element of originality in almost all the replies with regard to the way in which Rome had stated the questions. The insistence in the last two general question and in many of the particular questions on abuses, errors and difficulties amounted to an invitation to lament the excessive experimentalism of the early years following the Council, which in fact took place. However the replies also denounced the *restraining function of certain central organisms* of the Church hindering a more coherent development of the Council's intuitions on communion and collegiality.

5. THE DANEELS-KASPER REPORT TO THE SYNOD

The last part of the preparation and the first act of the synodal assembly was the reading of the report by G. Daneels, in the composition of which W. Kasper had co-operated to an unknown extent. The title, which attempted to synthesise programmatically the message of Council and synod, was: 'The Church, under the word of God, celebrates the mystery of Christ for the salvation of the world.'[15] This document is relevant to the analysis offered here to the extent that the opening report was intended to be the container of the 95 replies by the conferences,[16] given that it had been decided not to distribute the replies themselves to the members of the synod. If the replies had been distributed it would have enormously simplified and clarified the work and objectively increased communion between participants.

The introductory report (like the final one) is a *text which can be read in two ways.* It takes and assesses certain statements (which we found in our sample texts) of great theological weight and importance in the general context of the Synod's opening. It lists only some of them but accepts the assumption that the Council was a watershed: 'we cannot go back to things as they were before the Council' (p.5). But it denies the equation that 'what came after the Council came because of the Council' (p.6) and gives space to the preferential option for the poor (p.8 without the pharisaic addition of 'not exclusive'!), to the base communities, as a sign of 'hope for the universal Church' and not just for some particular churches (p.7). The same wise and positive attitude is shown in the passage on bishops' conferences (p.8) in which the *affectus collegialis* (LG23) is neatly referred to with regard to relations between bishops within conferences and between the various different conferences. Even more decisive was the statement that it was not possible to use the pastoral character of Vatican II to re-dimension it, because there was an intrinsic convergence between truth in pastoral activity and dogmatic truth.

But the impression immediately picked up by the press was also correct: *the report also carried more pessimistically conservative positions.* Some further examples: in two passages (p.4 and 20-21 in the Latin text) it says that the Council drew 'from the living springs . . . that is Holy Scripture and Tradition', thereby restoring the plural 'springs' for the Bible and tradition which had been reduced to one 'spring' or 'source' by DV. Moreover these two sources are also introduced later in inverse order as 'Holy Tradition and Holy Scripture' (p.21). At one point (p.9) in the matter of ecumenism it withdraws to the point of describing the Catholic task here as sharing in the 'motus unionis', and it looks suspiciously at mixed marriages (p.13). Partly following the Swiss conference, the report brands as absurd something which in fact no bishop had said, that is that the Church of before the Council was not the same Church as that after the Council, but in doing this it almost denies the possibility of making any distinction between before and after the Council. This was a distinction it had assumed earlier could be made (as we saw with regard to p.5) and it goes on to adopt the (more ambiguous than obvious) thesis that Vatican II is to be read 'in connection' (p.17) with the christological confessions of the early councils and then with Trent and Vatican I. It denies (p.17) the possibility of a new pentecost (an expression which Pope John XXIII had made central in his idea of the Council).

To sum up the Daneels-Kasper report in relation to our sample replies, it does present the opinion of the episcopal conferences, but in what appears to be a lawyer-like way: it notes the phenomena mentioned in these texts (as J. Komonchak also does in his introduction to the Extraordinary Synod) but it does not put them in any order or examine them. It simply expounds them. This happens particularly with the negative phenomena which thus assume an undue quantitative prevalence, even if this might not have been exactly what the speaker intended.[17] At the same time it does lead us to understand why the Synod did not follow that sort of line. The sense which the Synod fathers mostly attributed to Daneels' report was that which emerges as one of the most fruitful lines of the final report, that is to say, *keeping problems open instead of closing them in one way or another.* Thus Daneels' report's low profile and lack of order became the means by which the gold and the dross of the pre-synod debate among the bishops were passed on the the Synod, its resolutions and the way in which these resolutions were formally expressed.

6. CONCLUSION: THE BISHOPS RESPONSES AS EVIDENCE OF A JOURNEY THAT CONTINUES

Now at the end of this rapid survey of the texts written in preparation for the Synod, we can draw a few conclusions. As I write a few months after the closing of the Synod, it seems to have faded. It seems as if it is something over and done with in the minds of the top people in the Church (it is difficult to say whether this is for tactical reasons, either because of the way the Synod went or because of the real prevalence of new directions, or new pressures). In the light of these events should we conclude that we have given an undue importance to texts, the bishops' replies, which finally only lasted for one short day? I do not think so. I think that in fact the bishops' replies are paradoxically the most enduring fruit of the Synod, because they are the *product of an enquiry and evidence of a journey*—which even if it had lasted another forty years in the wilderness—will not return to its starting point. It is true that each reply read on its own may generally appear opaque, but read together they are evidence that the Council is not the end of the road for the Church but a light which burns too brightly to be put under a bushel. In the consultation of 451 which was mentioned at the beginning, Bishop Euippo who felt nervous about the dominance of a too philosophical approach to christological problems, coined the well known, deliciously evangelical phrase, that he had spoken *fisherly* and *not aristotley*, like a fisherman and not like an Aristotelian. Today we could also reproach the bishops' conferences for having missed some of the problems. We might even think that some of the replies which were not at our disposal may have been too submissive to certain Roman readings of the Council and under pressure to formulate immature opinions or judgments. But certainly these replies, *because* they were formulated in a *fishermanlike* way, show that the enormous value of Vatican II is not a desire or a hypothesis, but a reality, which is developing ever more coherently with the natural energy given to the Council with 'humble firmness of purpose'[18] by its father John XXIII and ever less influenced by the waverings of his ten thousand schoolmasters (1 Cor 4:15).

Translated by Dinah Livingstone

Notes

1. The members of the general secretariat, re-confirmed as a whole by vote of the Extraordinary Synod, which represents one of its greatest results, are: P.E. Arns J. Bernardin, J. Cordeiro, R. Etchegaray, M. Hermaniuk, S.F. Hamao, B. Hume, A. Lopez Trujillo, A. Lorscheider, C.M. Martini, S. Naidoo, J. Ratzinger, J. Schotte, J.L. Sin, H. Teissier, P. Zoungrana. On 7th March the secretary of state A. Casaroli had written a letter to the secretary of the Synod which tended to circumscribe the field of action of the next extraordinary assembly. Again on the 1st October. See L. Kaufmann 'Impulse zu weiterführender Erneuerung' in *Orientierung* 49 (1985) 226. The secretariat of state announced that the replies sent by the bishops' conferences were to be considered as reserved material not for publication, although the English and US bishops had already done so in *Origins* 15 (1985) 177–186 and 225–233 and the Italian conference did so later. See *Con il sinodo dei vescovi sulla strada del concilio* (Rome 1986).

2. In the letters sent by Tomko (who was succeeded by J. Schotte on 24th April) it says 'the following questions were compiled . . . after many consultations'. In fact the questions arose from the juxtaposition of requests by the Synod secretariat and by the curia.

3. On LG (*Lumen Gentium*) they were asked if the mystery of the Church had been received and put into practice in its double aspect as communion and hierarchical institution, although LG never uses the term 'institutio' for the Church!

4. This was about 70% of the conferences. However the counting of huge and very small conferences each as one and also the different levels of consultation used within the conferences make it impossible to say how many bishops were able to express their individual opinions. Nevertheless 95 is a significant number if we consider that only for the 1974 synod were there 98 replies, reducing to 86 for the 1977 synod (catechesis), 68 in 1980 (family), and a mere 59 in 1983 on penance.

5. The most consistent group of reports (15) are to be found in *Synode Extraordinaire. Célébration de Vatican II* (Paris 1986) (hereafter referred to as SE).

6. In 457–9 the Emperor Leo I set up a consultation of the bishops who had attended the Council of Chalcedon in 451. The product of this consultation was the so-called *Codex Encyclicus*. See A. Grillmeier *In Ihm und mit Ihm* (Freiburg 1975) 283–300.

7. These are reports sent in the name of conferences of various countries: Angola, Belgium, Brazil, Burkina-Faso and Nigeria, Canada, Chad, Korea, France, Gabon, Germany, Japan, Indonesia, England and Wales, Italy, Mahgreb, Low Countries, US, Scandinavia and Finland, Sudan, Switzerland, Zambia. The conference of Latin American religious also sent a report. Of course the text presented at the opening of the synod by G. Daneels, written together with W. Kasper, stands on its own. It was

published by the general secretariat of the Synod: *Ecclesia sub Verbo Dei Mysteria Christi celebrans pro Salute Mundi Relatio ad Synodi Episcoporum Coetum Extraordinariam anno 1985 habita* (Vatican City 1985). I have also used speeches by some of the fathers who spoke in the synodal chamber in the name of their own conference, presenting the content of their replies orally; for some of these the complete text was also made available. However I was unable to obtain replies from the Eastern European Bishops' conferences, although I explicitly asked for them.

8. See the acts of the Conference of European Bishops, who met in Rome in October to discuss secularisation in Europe. Although the theme had been programmed before the Synod, the debate turned into a sort of preparation for the Synod. Certain other appeals circulated with varying degrees of caution also went in this direction. See that in *Concilium* 181 (1985) ix–xii, that of the Ecumenical Council of Churches in SE 650–652 and that of the Institute for Religious Sciences of Bologna in *Rivista Ecclesiastica Brasilica* 45 (1985)/179 472–484.

9. For the convergences between Ratzinger's theses and Lefebvre's positions, see D. Menozzi 'Anti-concilio' in *Il Vaticano e la chiesa* ed. G. Alberigo-J. Jossua (Brescia 1985). Other neo-conservative circulars also shared Ratzinger's opinions. See *La Chiesa del Concilio* (Milan 1985) with essays by, among others, H.U von Balthasar and R. Buttiglione.

10. See e.g. contributions in *O Vaticano II e a Igreia Latino Americano* ed. J.O. Beozzo (Sao Paulo 1985) and also F. Biot *Lève toi et marche. Reponse a Ratzinger* (Paris 1985).

11. See *Il Vaticano II e la Chiesa*. ed. G. Alberigo-J. Jossua.

12. See the interviews collected from various sources: D. Del Rio *Memoria del Concilio* (Citta di Castello 1985); G.F. Svidercoschi *Intervista sul* Concilio (Rome 1985); 'Issues for the extraordinary Synod' *Origins* 5 (1985) 345–360 and also before this 97–101; 'Vatican II mode d'emploi' *Lettre* (1985)/325 with a piece by M.D. Chenu; see also Kaufmann, the article cited in note 1. On positions paradoxically close to Ratzinger see M. Winter *What happened to Vatican II* (London 1985).

13. I am thinking especially of the report of the international theological commission. It had been to a certain extent anticipated on the operative level by the decisions taken in the editing of the new CJC, which limited the decisional area of the conferences to marginal questions (see E. Corecco 'Aspetti della ricezione del Vaticano II nel Codice di diritto canonico' in *Il Vaticano II e la Chiesa* p. 33–397).

14. The request of the American conference taken up in the Daneels-Kasper report was for a 'little catechism' (cf. SE 192 and 107). On this issue J. Ratzinger intervened with *Die Krise der Katechese und ihre Überwindung* (Einsiedeln 1983). In this volume there are contributions by G. Daneels, reporter to the Synod, and P. Eyt, presenter of the document of the international theological commission to the synod: *L'unique Eglise du Christ* (Paris 1985). See the issue on 'Catechesi e catechismi' *Communio* (1983)/67 1–111. The Synod's decision had been conjectured, if not foretold, by J.M. Gimenez 'A proposito del proyecto de "catechism universal"' in *Scripta Theologica* 17 (1985) 245–254.

15. I quote and translate from the Latin text.

16. However, 10 were delivered at the opening of the Synod.

17. See W. Kasper in SE pp. 653–659, who explains many passages of Daneels' report, in which he tried to stress a globally positive view of the Council.

18. See John XXIII's speech of 25th January 1959 in Discorsi Messaggi Colloqui del S. Padre Giovanni XXIII (Vatican City 1960) I, p. 132. Certain expressions were

taken up at the opening of the Council. See G. Alberigo—A. Melloni 'L'allocuzione Gaudet Mater Ecclesia di Giovanni XXIII (11 ottobre 1962)' in *Fede Tradizione Profezia. Studi su Giovanni XXIII e sul Vaticano II* (Brescia 1984) p. 248. For John XXIII's speeches on the Council: *Giovanni XXIII. Il Concilio della speranza* ed. A. and G. Alberigo (Padua 1985).

James Provost

Reform of the Roman Curia

IN NOVEMBER 1985 three key institutes related to the Petrine ministry were evident in Rome: the college of cardinals met in an extraordinary meeting; among the topics of their discussion was the projected reform of the Roman curia;[1] and immediately following the cardinals' meeting, the extraordinary session of the Synod of Bishops convened. It is no coincidence that all three—*cardinals, curia, synod*—were in evidence: they not only are mentioned together in the same canon in the new code (c. 334); they also reflect the *three stages of development in the structures of the Apostolic See at Rome.*

Our study will review that historical development briefly; it will then examine some of the theoretical issues involved in both the reform of the curia and the Synod of Bishops, as well as some of the specific elements of the proposed curial reform. The study will conclude with some reflections on the relationship of Curia and Synod.

1. HISTORICAL BACKGROUND

Three distinct systems of organisation have been followed in the Apostolic See at Rome.[2] For approximately the first millennium organisational patterns typical of the other patriarchal sees were used. From the eleventh century reforms through the High Middle Ages, a system more characteristic of Western princely courts was adopted, primarily through the consistories or papal court sessions. With the Reformation and Counter-Reformation, a new system evolved, one of the first of the modern bureaucracies, which continues to be the characteristic organisation of the Apostolic See.

The *patriarchal system* was marked by a *synodal structure*. Decisions were made in consultation with the *presbyterium*, which at Rome included both presbyters and deacons. More important issues were taken up at regular councils, attended by bishops of the province or from even further away, and by the *presbyterium* of the City. A basic staff provided secretarial and accounting services at the papal palace.

When *reformers in the eleventh century* sought to reform Rome as well as the Western Church they built on this structure. Key presbyters, deacons, and neighbouring bishops had become '*cardinals*' in a liturgical sense,[3] and now became the central figures to assure reform. In the process, the whole structure began to change and patterned on a princely court, consistories of cardinals began to meet frequently—three times a week by the time of Innocent III (died 1218). While the same persons were involved as in the previous system, the spirit and manner of conducting business changed to follow more secular patterns.

This system proved incapable of responding to the *challenges of the sixteenth century Reformers*. Drawing on an existing practice of appointing ad hoc committees of cardinals to prepare issues for discussion in consistory, a *standing cardinalatial committee* (or 'congregation') was created to give ongoing attention to the dangers of heresy and schism—the Congregation of the Inquisition or Holy Office. Following Trent another permanent body of cardinals was established to oversee the implementation of the council's reforms—the Congregation of the Council.

Finally, in 1588 Sixtus V suppressed the ordinary consistories and turned over the regular concerns of the Apostolic See to *congregations of cardinals, divided according to ecclesiastical concerns* and those related to the government of the papal states.[4] Subsequent popes (Pius X in 1908, Paul VI in 1965-1969) have reformed the organisation of the system of congregations, but the system itself has remained in principle much as it was laid down by Sixtus V.

Technically, the *curia operates collegially* through policy and decision making committees of cardinals (and, since Paul VI, also including some diocesan bishops) who meet periodically in ordinary sessions, and annually in a plenary meeting (the *plenarium*). The chairman of the group, or prefect, also serves as the chief executive over the staff assigned to the congregation. Assisted by a secretary (usually an archbishop) and various other officials, the prefect is to implement the decisions of the congregation and also to deal with routine matters within the general principles set down by the full body. He and his assistants also prepare the agenda for meetings of the congregation and determine which matters belong on the agenda of regular or annual meetings.

The bishops at Vatican II called for some major reforms in the curia, and although Paul VI did introduce many of these reforms the bishops at the first extraordinary synod (1969) urged further reforms, especially in the curia's mode of operations and communications.[5]

2. THEORETICAL ISSUES

The institution of the Synod of Bishops has been subjected to various critiques relating to the *ecclesiology* which it embodies, its *relationship to supreme authority*, and its *mode of operation*. Interestingly, the same issues have been raised in regard to the Roman curia.

(a) Ecclesiological foundations

Although historically arising from a synodal or communal sense of Church, the curia has developed into a bureaucratic structure more characteristic of a civil state or 'perfect society'. Indeed, some of the most ardent proponents of the *societas perfecta* ecclesiology have been personnel of the Roman curia.[6]

At Vatican II the bishops called for the Curia to be reformed so it might be a more effective instrument 'for the good of the churches and in the service of the sacred pastors'.[7] In effect, the curia was to become integrated into the conciliar view of the communion of churches, respecting the fact that in and from the particular churches the one and catholic Church comes into being.[8]

Does this preclude an institutional dimension to the curia? It would seem not, for the very constitution of the Church includes an institutional dimension within the communion of churches. Yet the institutional aspect must always be seen *in service to the communion of faith, grace, charism and charity* which is central to the reality of the Church.[9]

(b) Relationship to supreme authority

The curia has developed as an instrumentality for the exercise of the Petrine ministry, and also as the agency for the Patriarch of the West to exercise his patriarchal functions. The mixing of these two dimensions has obscured not only the specific roles of the pope vis-à-vis the whole Church and within the Latin church; it has also led to *varying theories about the power of the curia itself*.[10]

Some medieval canonists saw in the College of Cardinals the continuation of the collegial dimension of the Apostles, with the diocesan bishops continuing the apostles' pastoral role.[11] There is still a sense in which the curia sees itself as a privileged continuation of responsibility for the whole Church, an echo of which has been detected by critics of the reform proposed for discussion in November 1985.

Vatican II recognised the curia as performing their duties in the pope's name and with his authority. In this sense it can be termed a papal institution, derived from the need of the pope to have assistants who aid him in carrying out his primatial and patriarchal (i.e., personal) responsibilities.

Others see the curia as participating in the collegial solicitude of bishops for the welfare of the whole Church. Cardinals are now also bishops; diocesan bishops serve on the congregations; major staff of most congregations are themselves members of the college of bishops. The pope himself always acts 'in communion' with the other members of the college (c. 333, §2), and so not apart or abstracting from the college of bishops.

Underlying these views is the *ongoing discussion of the agents of supreme power in the Church*. Some, including *Lumen gentium* and particularly the prefatory note to its third chapter, see this as two inadequately distinct agents: the pope acting alone (and hence the curia in his name and with his authority), and the pope and the rest of the bishops acting collegially. Others, including Rahner and Congar, have argued that the pope is always joined with the rest of the bishops in the college as their head, so that the true agent of supreme power is the college. At times the pope as head of the college may act singly, but never by some other power than that which the college itself enjoys.

A third view was held prior to the council but has not been in general circulation after *Lumen gentium*. It held that there was only one agent of supreme power, the pope, who sometimes acted alone and at other times (e.g., to add greater solemnity) joined with himself the bishops in a collegial act. Since the pope's involvement is the crucial determinant of whether an action is truly that of the college, this view argued the real power was solely papal.

These issues remain debated; the reform of the curia cannot resolve them, any more than the revised code attempted to. But the approach taken in the reform remains affected by the discussion, and necessarily will reflect one or another perspective. Some have sensed in the proposed *Lex peculiaris* an attempt to return to the pre-conciliar view of centralised papal power.

(c) Mode of operation

Conciliar criticism of the curia objected to *secret procedures, overlapping competencies*, and *conflicting responses* from various offices. The operations of the bureaucracy seemed cumbersome and ill-suited to the conditions of a world-wide Church. The criticism also faulted the limited personnel pool and the absence of a sense of the conditions in the churches around the world. What should be an administration by office was really an administration dependent on prestige and connections.

Paul VI followed through on many of the suggestions made during Vatican

II, reforming first the Holy Office[12] and then the entire curia.[13] However, after some experience with the new arrangement some observers found the results less than satisfactory in several respects.[14]

The procedures designed to resolve *conflict of competencies* (a major problem before the reforms of Pius X in 1908 and even subsequent to the 1917 code) did not seem adequate for the task. These procedures included the regular reunion of prefects by the secretary of state, and the principle of 'dialogue' among the interested congregations. One of the reasons these procedures were not adequate to the task was the continued overlapping of competencies in the various congregations. Shopping for the most favourable office to address an issue continued to be possible.

Coordination with conferences of bishops, as specified in Paul VI's reform, was being bypassed in practice by several congregations. The call of the 1969 Synod for working out more effective means of collaboration remains to be implemented.

Internationalisation of personnel, while stated in principle and desirable, was very difficult to achieve in practice. There was no 'Personnel Office' provided under *Regimini*, so recruitment of personnel (especially of staff within the various offices) was left to existing personnel. There was no *coherent personnel recruitment, training, or evaluation procedure*, nor was there an effective way in which to assure that in internationalising the curia the quality of personnel was not diminished (i.e., that the curia did not become the 'dumping ground' for persons who were not so desirable at home).

Although diocesan bishops who are not cardinals theoretically are full members of the congregations, in practice they had very little to say. Their involvement was often restricted to the annual plenary meetings, and even there the pastoral insights they could bring were not fully utilised.

From another front, there have been objections that placing the cardinal secretary of state in the position of presiding over the other department heads ran counter to the truly collegial character of the college of cardinals. Offices which were used to greater independence raised theoretical as well as practical difficulties to the new system.

3. THE 1985 *LEX PECULIARIS* REFORM

Five years after the publication of *Regimini* Paul VI asked the heads of the offices of the curia to evaluate their experience. In 1974 a commission of cardinals was named to revise *Regimini*, and at the death of Paul VI had practically finished its work. John Paul II asked the full college of cardinals to consider the curial reform, and the issue was discussed at special meetings of cardinals in 1979 and 1982.[15]

The cardinals asked for *more substantial reforms* than were being proposed, and in 1983 a new commission of curial officials was named to carry out the task.[16] The group began working in February 1984, and after fifty-three meetings produced the *Schema* which was discussed at the cardinals' meeting in November 1985.

The report which introduces the *Schema* reports on the *principles which were supposed to guide the work*. The pope himself laid down two fundamental considerations: to develop a greater pastoral direction, and to seek a greater correspondence between the structures of the Roman curia and diocesan curias in order to promote more effective collaboration. The commission added these principles: to produce a true and proper reform, not just a retouching of existing norms; to provide greater logic, clarity and coherence with regard to the competencies of the various departments so there would be more organic functioning within the curia; to require that the existence of any organism in the curia be justified by the three criteria of universality of the service to be rendered, real necessity, and efficiency; to implement the principles of subsidiarity and decentralisation, already used in the revision of the Code of Canon Law; and to use greater technical rigour, terminological precision and sobriety in the formulation of the norms, leaving details to later regulations each office is to adopt for its own operations.

(a) Overview of the *Schema*

The proposed reform is contained in 160 articles, beginning with a series of general norms and followed by sections for each of the thirty major offices proposed for the reformed curia. These are divided according to a more restricted set of classifications: those which exercise the *power of governance* (congregations and tribunals), and *others which ordinarily do not* (councils, commissions, and fiscal offices).

Many of the existing offices remain. Some have been given a *change in name* (Apostolic Secretariat for the Secretariat of State, Congregation for the Functions of Presbyters and Deacons, rather than Congregation for the Clergy; Congregation for Consecrated and Apostolic Life rather than Congregation for Religious and Secular Institutes, etc.). A new congregation is proposed for the apostolate of the laity, raising the existing Council for the Laity to the status of a congregation. Currently diplomatic relations are handled by the Council for the Public Affairs of the Church; it would become a congregation.

The *competencies of some congregations are to be changed*. For example, catechetics was a major concern of the Council of Trent; the pastor was charged to provide catechetical instruction in his parish. So, the Congregation for the Council, later changed to the Congregation for Clergy, developed a special section on catechetics. Under the proposed reform this would be moved to the Congregation for Catholic Education. Seminaries, now under the aegis of Catholic Education, would be transferred to Clergy, renamed Congregation for the Functions of Presbyters and Deacons; but strictly educational (as contrasted to formation) issues would remain with Catholic Education.

Although remaining a congregation rather than a tribunal, the Congregation for the Sacraments would take on the various cases dealing with sacraments now handled by itself and the Congregation for the Doctrine of the Faith (penance, orders, privilege of the faith marriage cases). The competencies of the Congregation for the Evangelisation of Peoples (Propaganda) would be reduced. The functions of the secretariats which developed during Vatican II (for the unity of Christians, for non-Christian religions, and for non-believers) would be curtailed due to their becoming councils, while the commission on 'Justice and Peace' (devoted to these specialised issues in the world) would be united with the Council 'Cor unum' which coordinates internal church subsidy to missionary works.

A major change in the general norms for all curial offices would recognise the *de facto* power exercised by the *second-in-command, the secretary*. This official would become a voting member of the congregation. The system of collegial government within congregations (in terms of the commission of cardinals and diocesan bishops charged with the highest policy and decision making functions of the office) would be weakened by recognising as 'congregation' the staff as well as the cardinals and bishops, and by reducing the requirements for plenary meetings to 'when it seems opportune'.

(b) Critiques of specific elements

On a theoretical level, the *Schema* has been criticised for *lacking a sound ecclesiological base*. As discussed above, there are a number of unresolved issues which affect an institution such as the Roman curia, so some criticism is to be expected from varying points of view. Yet the revision seems to have been so concerned about technical details that it not only ignores the ecclesiological issues but even fails to breathe the *pastoral sensitivity anticipated by the pope*.

Moreover, one of the basic principles of the reform has recently been called into question, namely *subsidiarity*. While this formed one of the principles for the revision of the Code of Canon Law and was peacefully accepted by the commission charged with drafting the *Schema* on curial reform, both at the

1985 cardinals' meeting and again in the extraordinary Synod the application of subsidiarity within the Church was challenged. Indeed, the final *Relatio* of the Synod put the question as to *whether* subsidiarity could be applied within the Church, not how or to what extent. This is a major shift in the question from the way it was discussed at the 1967 and 1969 Synods, and poses a special question to the proposed reform of the Curia.

On a *more practical level*, the proposed reform does not adequately address the concerns which gave rise to it. The pope wanted an organisation which would more readily relate to typical diocesan structures, yet the proposed reform continues the division of responsibilities traditional in the curia rather than corresponding to usual diocesan activities. For example, rather than locating in tribunals all those matters normally handled as 'cases' at the diocesan level, some are retained by the Congregation for the Sacraments. There is no dicastery of the curia which deals specifically with one of the key concerns in the Church today, *money*; the fiscal offices in the *Schema* are all internal to curial operations.

The *conflict of competencies* remains a problem, recognising that 'shopping' for a favourable office will continue. However, it must be admitted there may be no more realisable solution than the continued use of joint working groups proposed in the *Schema*.

The *Schema* does mention *coordination with conferences of bishops* a number of times, as well as the competence of both diocesan bishops and the conferences of bishops. Yet the practical suggestions of the 1969 synod on how to put this into effect have not been adopted, nor does there seem provision in the *Schema* for such mutual working out of a working relationship.

The *personnel question* is not addressed in the *Schema* beyond the same kind of statement concerning internationalisation that was in *Regimini*. In this sense the *Schema* fails to go deep enough to provide a *genuine reform* (which according to the principles for revision, it was supposed to do). The commission recognised this problem and left it up to higher authority to determine whether to institute an 'Office of Personnel'. Yet only when serious attention is given to the personnel system can other elements of the reform ever be effective.

The *involvement of diocesan bishops*, and indeed of cardinals who are diocesan bishops themselves, does not seem to be strengthened by the *Schema*. Plenary sessions, to which all must come, are not required even on an annual basis (they are to be held annually 'quantum fieri potest'—which means the moderator of the dicastery could determine that 'fieri non potest' for one or many years). If a dicastery does not have sufficient serious business to require an annual *plenaria* its existence would scarcely seem to qualify under the criteria adopted for the revision.

The proposed distinction between offices which exercise the power of governance and those which do not fails to take into consideration the more serious theoretical issues about the *nature of the power of the curia itself.* Moreover, it is not clear what criteria were used to apply the distinction in practice. For example, it is not clear what exercise of the power of governance is to distinguish the proposed Congregation for the Apostolate of the Laity from the Secretariat (or future Council) for Promoting the Unity of Christians. The latter's *Ecumenical Directory* remains the law in force in the Catholic Church today. ·

Indeed, the *treatment of the Secretariat for Promoting Christian Unity became the most controverted point* in the proposed reform. Many read the *Schema* as anti-ecumenical, an attempt not only to downgrade the office responsible for ecumenism at the level of the Holy See, but also to put so many restrictions on its leadership and operations as to make it ineffective.

4. CURIA AND SYNOD

The response to this final issue is illustrative of the continuing problems in *relationship between the college of cardinals as a distinct institution, the Roman curia and the synod of bishops.* Some at the cardinals' meeting reportedly objected to the proposed treatment of the Secretariat for Promoting the Unity of Christians, and the Synod placed concern for ecumenism as a high priority in the continued implementation of Vatican II. Repeated calls were made at the Synod for renewed efforts ecumenically.

Beneath this issue is the more fundamental one, that of the *relative importance of the synod and the Roman curia.* The underlying theory of governance in the Church is the interaction between executive responsibility and collective consultation at one level, and the creative tension between collegial and personal exercise of authority on another level.

Curial officials have repeatedly stated the synod is a consultative body, and that it is papal rather than collegial in nature. On the other hand, they have seen the curia as an executive, decision-making body, acting collegially in the name of the pope.

Conciliar proponents of the synod, however, viewed things somewhat differently. The synod was for some proponents an expression of the collegial solicitude of the members of the college of bishops, hence a form of collegiality although not in the fullest sense. It would assist the pope in the governance of the universal Church.[17] In one sense this would mean the curial offices might be asked to account for themselves to the bishops meeting in synod, and in practice there have been regular reports from various curial offices at the meetings of the synods.

However, neither view seems fully adequate to the *reality of the curia and the synod*. Each is a distinct institute and their *interrelationship is not clear either in theory or in law*. This is due partly to the various ecclesiological questions discussed earlier. It is also due to the fact that the two bodies are only inadequately distinct: the heads of the curial congregations are automatically members of the synod of bishops.

The experience in November 1985 does illustrate a need to resolve this relationship. Currently the college of cardinals, the Roman curia, and the synod of bishops share many of the same members, but do not address the same agenda in a coordinated fashion. The result is a *scattering of resources* and, as illustrated through the reaction to the *Schema* for the reform of the Curia, a failure to focus effectively on some of the real issues. A Church with increasingly limited resources but expanding needs cannot afford such a luxury.

Notes

1. The *Schema Legis Peculiaris de Curia Romana* (Typis Polyglottis Vaticanis, 1985) was circulated *subsecreto* to the cardinals and presidents of conferences of bishops for comment prior to the November 1985 cardinalatial meeting.

2. See N. Del Re *La Curia Romana: Lineamenti storico-giuridici*, Rome[3] 1970: he divides the history into five periods, but the later reforms of the bureaucracy did not change its basic nature.

3. See S. Kuttner '*Cardinalis*: The History of a Canonical Concept' *Traditio* 3 (1945) 129–214.

4. See Sixtus V, apostolic constitution *Immensa aeterni Dei*, 22 January 1588.

5. On the 1969 Synod, see E. Farhat 'De Primo Extraordinario Synodi Coetu (1969)' *Monitor Ecclesiasticus* 97 (1972) 3–23, esp. 9–15.

6. See, for example, A. Ottaviani *Institutiones Iuris Publici Ecclesiastici* 2 vols., Rome[4] 1958. At the time of Vatican II Ottaviani was one of the most forceful exponents of the *societas perfecta* understanding of Church.

7. *Christus Dominus* 9.

8. *Lumen gentium* 23.

9. John Paul II, apostolic constitution *Sacrae disciplinae leges*, 25 January 1983: *AAS* 75/II (1983) xi.

10. See discussion by K. Morsdorf in his commentary on *Christus Dominus* in *Commentary on the Documents of Vatican II* ed. H. Vorgrimler II (New York 1968) pp. 210–212. (*Lexikon für Theologie und Kirche*, supplementary volumes.)

11. See Y. Congar 'Notes sur le destin de l'idée de collégialité épiscopale en occident au moyen age (VIIe-XVIe siècles)' in *La collégialité épiscopal: Histoire et théologie* (Paris 1965) pp. 99–129.

12. Paul VI, motu proprio *Integrae servandae* 7 December 1965: *AAS* 57 (1965) 952-955.

13. Paul VI, apostolic constitution *Regimini Ecclesiae universae* 15 August 1967: *AAS* 59 (1967) 885-928.

14. See J. Sanchez Y Sanchez 'Pablo VI y la Reforma de la Curia Romana' *Revista Espanola de Derecho Canónico* 22 (1966) 461-478; 23 (1967) 85-107; *idem* 'La Constitution Apostolique 'Regimini Ecclesiae Universae' 'six ans après' *Année Canonique* 20 (1976) 33-66.

15. Although not considered formal consistories at the time, the introduction to the *Schema Legis Peculiaris* terms both meetings 'consistories'.

16. The commission members have been identified as: Cardinal Sabattani (Apostolic Signatura), president; Bishops E. Gagnon (Council for the Family), R. Castillo Lara (Code Commision), G. Coppa (Secretariat of State), Z. Grocholewski (Apostolic Signatura), and Monsignors A. Ranaudo and G. Marra (Administration of the Patrimony of the Apostolic See).

17. See discussion in Morsdorf, the article cited in note 10, pp. 214-219.

Ronaldo Muñoz

The Ecclesiology of the International Theological Commission

LAST YEAR the International Theological Commission produced, with an eye to the Extraordinary Synod of Bishops, a document entitled 'The One Church of Jesus Christ: Selected Themes in Ecclesiology on the Occasion of the 20th Anniversary of the End of the Second Vatican Council'.[1] I have been asked to produce a short theological commentary on this document *from the viewpoint of the people of God in Latin America*.

It is somewhat pretentious for a theologian from the periphery, involved in the pastoral service of an oppressed people, to attempt a critical commentary on a document which is so important both because of its subject and the status and number of its authors. Accordingly I have ventured to undertake this commentary, with due modesty, only after noting the Euro-centric and hierarchical bias of the ecclesiology presented in the document. Having studied the text, I felt that, while time did not permit a detailed and argued commentary, it could be useful to pose some fraternal questions to the authors.

Here I shall discuss what seem to me the three main concerns of the Theological Commission's document, indicating in passing its *deficiencies from our Latin American viewpoint*.

1. THE CATHOLIC CHURCH AS THE THEOLOGICAL AND SAVING CENTRE OF THE WORLD AND HISTORY

The first striking feature of the text is its *heavily Church-centred attitude*, visible both in its view of the Church's relation to Jesus and of its relation to

37

humanity. The Church does not so much appear in the text as a disciple of Jesus and sacrament of Jesus, Jesus Christ appears as precursor, founder and animator of the ecclesial institution. The Church, again, does not appear as a servant of humanity in function of a reign of God whose dynamic traverses history, but humanity appears as a background and material for the Church, understood as the realisation of the kingdom of God here and now on earth.[2] In this double relationship, with Jesus and with humanity—a key relationship for the Church's consciousness and mission—we thus note a *regression from the process of 'decentralising' or 'conversion to God in human beings'*, which was recognised as the great originality of the Church which emerged from Vatican II.[3]

It is true that towards the end of the document there is a *rich and quite subtle chapter on 'The Church as the Sacrament of Christ'*.[4] Here it is explained that the Church is a sacrament in the sense of the presence of the 'mystery' of God's love in history, and as the deep reality of the 'communion' of God with human beings and of human beings with each other.[5] We are told that the Church, as the 'body' and 'sacrament' of Christ, is identified with him and makes him present; but, as the 'people' of the New Covenant and 'bride' of Christ, the Church cannot be confused with Jesus himself, but looks towards him and journeys to meet him. Even in this context, however, there is no mention, as we might have hoped, of the practical following of the historical Jesus with his options, life-style and ministry. There is, though, a reference to the practical responsibility of the Christian community for enabling the Church effectively to become the sacrament of Christ among human beings and for their salvation. And at the same time there is a recognition that in reality the mediation of this 'sacrament' operates for 'certain' people, while 'others' are associated with the mystery of Christ 'through the holy Spirit and in a way which only God knows'.[6] In the case of these others, however, this seems to refer only to an interior communion and eternal salvation. There is not even a suggestion that their lives and 'temporal' tasks and those of the members of the Church may also bring into being and signify in their way the reign of God through his Spirit, that they may be taking forward, as we believe, a total development and liberation of human beings which point to their full realisation at their definitive meeting with the God of Jesus Christ, who is the God of life and history.[7]

In the next chapter of the document, on 'The One Church of Jesus Christ', the *same ecclesio-centrism reappears in strength*—as a 'Catholic' caveat towards the *ecumenical movement*.[8] Here the Theological Commission maintains that 'all God's saving work in the world is related to the (Catholic) church because in it the means for growing in the life of Christ have reached their pinnacle and perfection'. The reference to these 'means' in practice means the ministry and teaching of the hierarchy.[9] From our viewpoint on the periphery, such a statement seems to me exaggerated, or at least one-sided. We prefer to say, conversely, that everything in the Church—starting with its ministries—is related and directed to the life of faith and love of the believing people, whose witness in its turn is directed—as a 'sacrament' at its service—to God's saving work in the world.

Finally, the last chapter, 'The Eschatological Character of the Church', speaks of the relation kingdom: Church as a relation between the present earthly Church and the future heavenly Church. It asserts the identity of the latter with the future fulness of the kingdom of God. As regards the present, it insists that the kingdom itself is already mysteriously present in the pilgrim Church, which is its 'seed and beginning on earth'.[10]

In a way which we find surprising, the document does not discuss the kingdom of God which here and now surpasses the Church and, with the Spirit's dynamism, permeates the whole space of human activity and history. Still less is it able to discuss the service the Church should give to this kingdom of God which is active in our peoples' journeying.[11] The text simply states, as it were in passing, that outside the social body of the Catholic Church the kingdom is present as 'an attachment—at least implicit—to this Church'. It seems that the search for truth, the practice of generous love and the struggle for justice which take place in human life and history do not, for the authors, contain any theological density, any content or implication of the reign of God, except in so far as that life and those strivings may guide individuals towards the Catholic Church.

2. THE STRUCTURE OF THE CHURCH AS A DIVINE INSTITUTION

The Theological Commission's document also lays heavy stress on the Church as an institution 'of divine right'.

The text begins with the foundation of the Church by Jesus Christ with its 'permanent and definitive fundamental structure'.[12] It then applies to the Church the concept of 'people of God', but interpreting it as one of the various theological images or symbols of the 'mystery' of the Church.[13] It goes on to discuss the two dimensions of the Church, as '*mystery*' and '*historical subject*', but explains the latter in an ontological and existential sense as referring to the everyday lives of believers, without giving adequate recognition to the dimension of *a collective subject* which journeys, acts, takes different forms and enters into conflicts in a contingent history.[14]

The document speaks of 'people', 'community' and 'institution' at a symbolic level which appears sociologically neutral. In reality, however, these abstract concepts are taken over to serve as theological attributes of the existing ecclesiastical institution. In this sense the text shows an inability to envisage real ecclesial communities and believing peoples which are *not mere projections of the hierarchico-sacramental institution*. The authors are unable to reflect any experience of faith nourished in actual communities, or of hope shared in the movement of historical peoples. They seem to ignore the fruitfulness and the difficulties of an ecclesiology which seeks, in faithfulness to the Gospel, to reflect an ecclesial reality which is complex and full of interactions: on the one hand the hierarchical institution, with its authority and bonds of universal communion, on the other a whole network of communities of different sorts, more or less prophetic, in which fellowship is lived and Jesus Christ is celebrated and proclaimed in tangible ways, and finally the broad mass of the believing people who are barely aware of the hierarchical institution and only sporadically receive the service of an evangelising community, but who in their lives and fellowship in their own way keep the memory of Jesus Christ and wait for his coming.[15]

This inadequacy must be connected with the markedly *Euro-centric perspective of the document*. It contains no serious reference to the oppressed majority of the world's population, nor is there any attempt to make a theological link between the 'people of God' and the 'people of the poor'. Not only is there no reference to the 'church of the poor', but the mission of the Church is also discussed with no reference to the evangelical option for the poor.[16] Moreover, the text talks of 'enculturation' and the 'evangelisation of cultures' as a challenge to the 'non-European' churches, apparently supposing that European ecclesiastical forms and European theology are *per se* 'Catholic'. In the same spirit it talks of the promotion of justice as an 'element of enculturation'.[17]

The Euro-centric perspective of the document is also shown in its treatment as part of 'the essential structure of the Church' of the *identification made by the Code of Canon Law (see c. 368) of the 'particular church'* with the diocese. Vatican II described the 'particular church' as 'linked to its pastor (in this case the bishop) and gathered together by him in the holy Spirit through the Gospel and the Eucharist',[18] but this identification does not take account of the fact—frequent in the Third World—that the bishop presides at a distance over a people dispersed over huge areas or crowded into gigantic cities in such a way that the proclamation of the Gospel and the celebration of the Eucharist—when they are possible at all—are experienced in smaller communities through the ministry of the presbyters.

It is not that the document ignores the distinction which always has to be made in the Church between its essential and permanent structure (*de iure divino*) and its actual, variable form and organisation (*de iure ecclesiastico*). In fact, it states the distinction clearly, and explains that 'the essential structure is always found embodied in an actual form, without which it would have no existence. For this reason the actual form is not neutral in relation to the essential structure, and must be able to express it in a given situation faithfully and effectively'.[19]

Now the only application of this principle which the document works out is related to *episcopal conferences*. It explains that they are only one particular historical form, and in themselves a transitory one, of the essential structure or principle of *ecclesial collegiality*.[20] However, the document does not mention other particular institutional 'forms' or practices—such as the Roman curia, cardinals, nuncios and the centralised and autocratic appointment of bishops—which are increasingly appearing to be *in contradiction with episcopal conferences*, and perhaps even with the principle of episcopal collegiality. In this point the ecclesiology of the Theological Commission shows a particularity which is not merely European, but Roman or curial.

At a more basic level the document insists on the 'essential structure' of the *Eucharist*, presided over by an ordained minister, as the vital centre of the actual ecclesial community.[21] But it seems to be unaware that in practice for the vast majority of our believing peoples this essential principle is being turned into a dead letter by the *exclusive retention of an 'historical form' of the presbyteral ministry*—with the discipline of celibacy and a training based on monastic and university models—which does not correspond to the culture of most of our people.

3. THE HIERARCHY AS 'VERTICAL' PRIESTHOOD AND AUTHORITY OVER THE BELIEVING PEOPLE

The Theological Commission recognises that the common priesthood of believers and the 'worship of life' have deep roots in the New Testament and had more or less disappeared from Catholic theology, and that, conversely, the 'ministerial or hierarchical' priesthood does not appear in the New Testament and took on great importance in later tradition.[22] It does not recognise, however, that the clergy and the priestly cult, so important in the religion of the Old Testament, were abolished by the New, nor that *later ecclesiastical practice and theology in large part restored the Old Testament clergy and priesthood* in so far as they concentrated 'the ministry' or religious power, and in so far as they associated themselves with 'authority' or political power.

The document uses the terms 'ministry', 'priesthood' and 'hierarchy' in rapid sequence as though all three had the same meaning and an equally solid basis in the New Testament.[23] What in fact it does is to accumulate or concentrate the theological content of 'ministry' and 'priestly worship' in the hierarchy, as a specific structure and group within the Church.

In relation to *ministry*, from the twofold fact that Jesus called together the infant Church and appointed the apostles as pastors, and that in the Church structure and life cannot be separated, the document appears to conclude that the Catholic episcopate must *iure divino* concentrate in itself monopolistically and identify itself in an exclusive way with the 'true ministry of the community'.[24] One wonders where this leaves the freedom of the Spirit to call forth new life, charisms and ministries in the community, and the duty of pastors to excercise obedient discernment and 'not to quench the Spirit'.[25]

In relation to *priesthood*, the document insists that the offering of the 'worship of life' reaches its fulness in the liturgical worship presided over by an ordained minister, the only person who can 'insert this worship into the sacrifice of the Son'.[26] It thus seems to suggest that the faithful have no communion in the sacrifice of Christ outside the liturgy and that there is no liturgy strictly speaking if it is not presided over by an ordained minister. In so doing it stresses a 'mediating' or 'representative' role for the hierarchy between God and the faithful people,[27] as though the people could not enjoy a direct communion with the one Mediator, Jesus Christ, through whom God acts in the life of the people and the people have direct access to God.[28]

Lastly, in the *specific vocation of the laity* it stresses sacramental participation and the witness of faith—in a way which makes this vocation appear derived and secondary within 'the hierarchically ordered people of God'— more than the prior and properly lay aspect, the experience of faith and the practice of love in everyday life.[29]

The Theological Commission presents us with a markedly *clerical and hierarcho-centric ecclesiology* which, it is to be hoped, will provoke a crisis— for the good of the Church—at the next world synod, to be devoted to the laity.

Translated by Francis McDonagh

Notes

1. International Theological Commission (ITC) *L'unique Eglise du Christ*, report prepared for the Synod by Mgr P. Eyt, preface by Cardinal J. Ratzinger (Paris 1985). Quotations here are translated from the author's Spanish (trans.).

2. ITC, Ch. 1; see Chs 8–10.

3. See Paul VI, Closing speech at Vatican II, on the religious significance of the Council; John-Paul II *Redemptor Hominis* 11–14.

4. ITC, Ch. 8.

5. See Vatican II *Lumen Gentium* 1,9,48.

6. See Vatican II *Lumen Gentium* 14, 16; *Ad Gentes* 7; *Gaudium et Spes* 22.5.

7 See Paul VI *Populorum Progressio* 20,21; Second General Conference of the Latin American Episcopate *Medellín Document* Introduction 4–6; Justice 3–5; Catechesis 4–7; Third General Conference of the Latin American Episcopate *Puebla Document* 87–90; 127–41; 470–506. On the spread of this understanding of the faith in Latin American Catholicism, see R. Muñoz *Nueva Conciencia de la Iglesia en América Latina* (Salamanca 1974) pp 205–39.

8. ITC, Ch. 9.

9. ITC, pp. 60–61.

10. See Vatican II *Lumen Gentium* 5.

11. See Vatican II *Lumen Gentium* 9, 36; *Gaudium et Spes* 34–39; *Puebla Document* 193, 226–29, 274, 787, 789, 796–99.

12. ITC, Ch. 1.

13. ITC, Ch. 2.

14. ITC, Ch. 3.

15. See *The Challenge of Basic Christian Communities* ed. J. Eagleson and S. Torres (New York 1981); R. Muñoz *La Iglesia en el Pueblo: Hacia una ecclesiología latinoamericana* (Lima 1983), with bibliography. A. Quiroz *Ecclesiología en la Teología de la Liberación* (Salamanca 1983), with bibliography.

16. See *Medellín Document* Poverty; *Puebla Document* Message 3; 31–42, 87–90, 190, 297, 452, 643, 733, 973–75, 1134–65; John-Paul II, speeches in Latin America, *passim*; *Laborem Exercens* 8.

17. ITC, Ch. 4.

18. ITC, p. 33; see Vatican II *Christus Dominus* 11.

19. ITC, pp. 33–34.

20. ITC, pp. 36–38.

21. ITC, pp. 42, 46–50.

22. ITC, pp. 45–46.

23. ITC, Chs 6–7.

24. ITC, pp. 40–41.

25. See Vatican II *Lumen Gentium* 4, 9, 12.

26. ITC, p. 48.

27. ITC, p. 50.

28. See Matt. 11:25–27; 23:1–12; John 14:23–26; Acts 2:14–18; 1 Cor. 2:10–16; 1 Tim. 2:5; Heb. 12:18–24; 1 John 1:1–3; Vatican II *Lumen Gentium* 9, 12; *Sacrosanctum Concilium* 5–8.

29. ITC, pp. 50–52.

PART II

The Meeting

Jan Kerkhofs

The Members of the Synod

THE CHURCH is not a democracy. A synod is not a parliament. Statistical norms cannot be used to measure how representative the representatives of local Churches and of groups and sectors within the Church are. Beyond this, what democracy is really representative? How does one give equal play to quantity and quality—and who determines the latter?

On the other hand, a collegial Church authority that does not to some extent reflect the cultural variety (with its numerical implications) and the pluralism of tendencies in the people of God as at present constituted lacks credibility even in the eyes of believers. Decisions taken by an authority of this kind have little chance of encountering docile agreement. The dramatic conflicts and divisions within the Church in the past remain a hard lesson here.

Probably it is always impossible to reach the right balance between a historically determined hierarchy and an equally historically evolving and multi-cultural people of God. But it is what we are striving for. Vatican II wanted the internationalisation of the Curia, a rejuvenation of the leadership, more say in appointments for priests and faithful. When the Roman Synod of bishops was being established attention was drawn to the complementary representativity of the Eastern churches (numerically they are over-represented, but theologically this is justified), the bishops' conferences (even the smallest countries are represented and the influence of the largest ones is limited), the superiors of men's religious orders (with the freedom and universality they enjoy), the Curia (which strengthens the pope's position), and finally and above all the pope himself (with his ability to nominate additional members up to 15 per cent of the total). This last category enables the pope to restore any imbalance that may arise between different tendencies or countries but also provides him with the opportunity of strengthening his own position. In addition one should not forget that in particular the cardinals, who always make up a high proportion of synod members, but also all diocesan bishops are naturally appointed by the pope. Finally all the members are clerics (with the exception of a few synods where one non-clerical religious was a member). All women are *ipso facto* excluded. Women and lay-people can only be present as experts or 'auditors'. Their selection is entirely dependent on the choice of the pope and the Curia. The synod is not simply a Church affair but also a political event.

It is against this background that the following rather statistical analysis needs to be located. It should also be taken into account that the synods of 1969 and 1985 were extraordinary synods, i.e. at them the bishops' conferences were represented only by their presidents and not by elected delegates and that the group of religious superiors was reduced to three.

Table 1: The representation of bishops from local churches.*

Synod	Europe	Africa**	Asia	North America	South America	Australasia
1967	40	31	17	8	34	5
1969	22	28	14	2	22	4
1971	39	32	20	8	36	5
1974	40	33	22	8	36	5
1977	40	31	19	8	36	5
1980	41	36	22	8	35	5
1983	39	37	24	8	37	5
1985	24	33	17	2	22	4

Some official lists give divergent figures according to whether those invited are counted or those actually present.
**Before and after the establishment of the Ethiopian bishops' conference their representatives were not counted here but among the Eastern churches.*

Some facts are noticeable. The representation of non-Western countries at ordinary synods is more important than that of Western countries (Europe and North America), for example 64.4% as against 35.5% in 1967 and 68.6% as against 31.3% in 1983. In the case of extraordinary synods the representation of non-Western countries is even more significant, with 73.9% as against 26.0% in 1969 and 74.5% against 25.4% in 1985. If we also take account of the representatives of the Eastern churches (whose numbers are almost exactly the same, give or take one, at all synods) the proportion of non-Western countries drops very slightly at the extraordinary synods (to 73.5% in 1969 and to 73.2% in 1985) whereas it increases slightly at the ordinary synods (for example to 65.5% in 1967 and to 68.9% in 1983).

During the pontificate of John Paul II the curial group has become more

Table 2: The representation of members nominated by the pope and of the Curia.

Synod	Papal nominees				Curia			
	1 Total	2 West	3 Non-west	4 Curia	5 Total	6 West	7 Non-west	Total 4 plus 5
1967	25	21	4	8	14	13	1	22
1969	18	14	4	6	19	18	1	25
1971	25	15	10	4	19	18	1	23
1974	21	12	9	4	17	15	2	21
1977	18	10	8	5	17	15	2	22
1980	24	14	10	4	19	15	5	23
1983	23	11	12	3	20	17	3	23
1985	21	10	11	2	24	18	6	26

internationalised, with an increase in the number of non-Westerners. There was a marked decline in the Italian representation, from 16 in 1967 to 10 in 1985. On the other hand the total of members of the Curia remained pretty constant. It is noticeable that the highest numbers were recorded at the two extraordinary synods.

Invited non-members

From the 1971 synod a number of people other than the special secretaries have sometimes been present at meetings of the synod without being members of it. Thus the 1971 synod included 11 experts, the so-called assistant secretaries, who included two lay-women and four laymen, as well as 26 priest-auditors. The 1977 synod drew 13 experts, five of whom (including three sisters) were women. The 1980 synod (on the family) mustered 10 experts, including one married couple, and 43 auditors, including 16 married couples, two lay-women and three sisters—a total of 22 women. The 1983 synod (on reconciliation) was attended by 14 experts and nine auditors, including two sisters. The 1985 synod brought together 12 experts, 15 auditors (eight of whom, including five sisters, were women), 10 observers from other Churches (all of whom were men), and 15 special guests, most of whom were cardinals and archbishops who were now retired but who had taken part in Vatican II: there were also five other invited guests, one of whom was a woman. The opening of the synod to non-members, begun by Paul VI,[1] was confirmed by John Paul II.

The synod council

On 28 November 1969, immediately after the 1969 synod, Paul VI decided to set up a council attached to the synod's general secretariat.[2] On the first occasion this council was elected by postal vote by the members of the previous synod. Subsequently the council was elected by successive synods. It meets only occasionally: most of its members live a long way from Rome. The council only exists formally between meetings of the synod and has no juridical competence during meetings of the synod. A new council is elected after each synod. After some hesitation the council elected by the 1983 synod was confirmed in its function by the 1985 synod until that of 1987. This brief survey makes it abundantly clear that in comparison with the Curia this council carries little weight.

Its limited competence is diminished still further by the fact that few of its members serve for more than one term of office. Thus Cardinal Cordeiro from Pakistan is the only member to have been consistently re-elected since 1969, followed by Cardinal Lorscheider from Brazil, who was first elected in 1971. Cardinal Wojtyla served from 1971 until his election as pope in 1978. Cardinal Bernardin from the USA has been re-elected continuously since he was first elected in 1974. The following group (three from each continent) was elected in 1983: Bernardin, Lorscheider, Arns; Zoungrana, Naidoo, Teissier; Sin (the only one to be elected on the first round), Cordeiro, Hamao; Hume, Martini, Etchegaray. The pope supplemented this list with Ratzinger, Lopez Trujillo and Hermaniuk. At the 1985 synod some of the above were automatically members, as presidents of bishops' conferences or as curial cardinals. Of the others only Cardinal Lorscheider found himself on the list of papal nominees: it happened that Cardinals Arns, Bernardin, Martini and Sin were absent.

The 1985 synod compared with the Council

As far as is known no detailed study has been made of the relations between Western and non-Western representation at Vatican II. There were shifts in numbers between the sessions. Probably more important is the fact that between 1960 and 1965 the number of foreign missionary bishops in non-Western countries was still so high that one could not yet talk of non-Western cultures being represented.[3] The Italian predominance was then impressive: Italy provided 43% of the European residential bishops while having only 19% of Europe's Catholics. Beyond this 15 of the 20 curial cardinals were Italian, as were nine of the 11 members of the preparatory commission. According to R. Aubert the European delegation at Vatican I was also two-fifths Italian and two-thirds of the consultors and all the secretaries were Italian. Of roughly 700 council fathers at Vatican I roughly 60% were European.

If we compare the distribution at the start of Vatican II and at the 1985 synod, we find some striking changes:

The representation of Western and non-Western countries at Vatican II and at the 1985 synod.

Vatican II Bishops invited[4]		Catholic population[5]	1985 synod Bishops' conferences represented		Total synod members		Catholic population[6]
Total	%	%	Total	%	Total	%	%
Western countries:							
1426	50	53.1	26	27.9	60	36.3	41
Non-Western countries:							
1425	50	46.8	67	72.0	105	63.6	59
Total:							
2851	100	100	93	100	165	100	100

Both the majority of the Catholic population and the majority of synod members belonged in 1985 to non-Western countries, in contrast to the situation at Vatican II. Beyond this all the representatives of non-Western bishops' conferences (with one exception) were in 1985 natives of their countries. This favourable ratio for non-Western countries was admittedly modified by the synod members that were not representing a bishops' conference, though here too the proportion of non-Westerners was much higher than at the Council. The decline in Westerners will develop further in the future. The Catholic Church's centre of gravity, both with regard to its leadership and with regard to its members, is shifting steadily towards what is called the southern hemisphere, particularly towards Latin America and above all Brazil. A Vatican III could therefore have considerable surprises in store.

Translated by Robert Nowell

Notes

1. From 12 September 1963 onwards lay auditors took part in the Council.
2. Africa, Asia, America (North and South), and Europe had three members each, supplemented by three members to be nominated by the pope, making a total of 15.
3. Thus just before the Council there were 54 residential and 11 titular missionary bishops from the Netherlands alone.

4. The bishops invited according to *Het Concilie* II: 3, 1961–62 (Katholiek Archief, Amersfoort 1962) pp. 186–198. In fact 2,778 council fathers were summoned of whom roughly 2,200 took part regularly.

5. Following *Bilan du Monde* (Casterman 1964) I, p. 38 (data for 1958–60).

6   *Annuarium Statisticum Ecclesiae 1983* (Rome 1985) p. 41.

Joseph Komonchak

The Theological Debate

THE EXTRAORDINARY Synod of 1985 issued only two documents, a 'Message to the People of God' and a 'Final Report'. Of these the second is the more important and has rightly received most attention. By itself, however, it is not an adequate or even accurate gauge of the theological issues discussed at the Synod. Furthermore, even properly to interpret and evaluate its conclusions, one must refer to the pre-synodal responses of the churches, the Initial and Second Reports of Cardinal Danneels, and the summaries of the discussions in the hall and in the language-groups. This essay will attempt such a review, concentrating particularly on the ecclesiological issues of the debate.[1]

1. THE FRAMEWORK OF THE DISCUSSION

The discussion was given an initial framework in the letter sent by Archbishop Jozef Tomko to those who had a right to take part in the Synod. Following the advice of the consilium of the Synod, this letter asked the churches to concentrate on the four conciliar Constitutions and to answer *four questions*: (1) How was the Council made known, received and implemented? (2) What benefits did the churches derive from the Council? (3) What errors or abuses have there been and what was done and still needs to be done to correct them? (4) What difficulties, new or old, remain in the way of an implementation of the Council, and how can they be met?

In the Final Report, these four questions are fitted into a *three-fold description of the Synod's purposes*: to celebrate, verify, and further the Second Vatican Council. But, after devoting a single sentence each to celebration and verification, the Final Report devotes almost all of its remaining text to the *further promotion of the Council* by identifying difficulties and proposing various measures, theological, spiritual and practical, to meet them. In other words, it is the last two of Archbishop Tomko's questions which guide the Final Report, while almost all that was said before and during the Synod in response to the first two questions is not represented.

In good part this imbalance can be explained by the dynamics of the Synodal debate and by the circumstances of the redaction of the Final Report. Cardinal Danneels' Initial Report mentioned the immense effort that the churches had made to make the Council known and effective and it devoted several pages to the churches' reports of its positive fruits. His Second Report, at the end of the first week's discussion, noted that the Council had been unanimously celebrated as a great gift of God to the Church; but his emphasis, somewhat understandably, fell on what yet remained to be done both at the Synod and in the life of the Church. He explained three times that, for that reason, he would not repeat the descriptions of the benefits of the Council which he had made in his Initial Report.

The agenda suggested to the language-groups was precisely to *concentrate on present problems and on how to meet them*. This is at least part of the reason why, as several observers remarked, the reports of these groups were so much more negative in tone and direction than those of the first week's interventions. Concentrating on present difficulties and their solutions, the groups could simply take for granted what had already been 'celebrated' and 'verified'.

Moreover, the Final Report was written in close dependence on the Second Report and on the summaries of the conclusions of the language-groups. Whole sections of it are taken from one or another of these sources and without much concern for synthesis or even coherence, for which in any case there was scant time in the last days of the Synod. For this reason, the Final Report is much more *a summary of the second week's work than of the first week's* and of the reports submitted by the churches before the Synod. Hence, the importance of placing the Final Report in the *context of the pre-synodal reports and the synodal discussions*. The Final Report, along with the Synod's 'Message to the People of God', may be the only document on which the Synod voted as a body, but without the earlier discussion, its analysis of present problems and proposals for their solution presupposes the 'celebration' and 'verification' of the Council which the Final Report barely acknowledges.

2. THE ECCLESIOLOGICAL ISSUES

I will focus the analysis of the theological debate on two primary ecclesiological issues raised in the Final Debate: the *basic notion of the Church* and the *realisation of ecclesial communion*. The positions of the Final Report will be illumined by comparison with earlier stages of the synodal discussions.

(a) The Notion of the Church

The Final Report emphasises two fundamental notions of the Church: *'mystery' and 'communion'*. It presents the first as an antidote to the reductive anthropology it identifies with secularism and as a way of responding to the signs of a return to the sacred which it finds today. The Church is mystery as participating in the mystery of God in Christ and in the Holy Spirit. On the basis of this mystery, the Final Report calls for greater attention to the Council's chapter on the universal call to holiness. This paragraph points to a dimension of the Church which some pre-synodal reports and some interventions in the synod hall had said needs to be recovered in the Church.

But two aspects of the Report's comments on mystery need to be noted. 'The whole importance of the Church', it begins, 'derives from her connection with Christ. The Council described the Church in different ways: as the People of God, the Body of Christ, the Bride of Christ, the Temple of the Holy Spirit, the family of God. These descriptions of the Church complement one another and must be understood in the light of the mystery of Christ or of the Church in Christ.' This is the *only reference to 'People of God'* in the whole of the Final Report, and here it appears as simply one notion among many. From the Final Report one could suspect that 'People of God' had been the title of a whole chapter of *Lumen Gentium*, that it had served as one of the architectonic themes of the Council's ecclesiology, and that it had been introduced precisely as an articulation of the very mystery of the Church in the time between Ascension and Parousia. Somewhere between the Council and the Synod, it came to be believed that to stress the mystery of the Church required one to underplay the Church as the People of God, to the point that some observers even speak of the Synod's having 'entombed' the expression 'People of God'.

Neither the pre-synodal responses nor the synodal interventions required this development. Several of them indicated how significant and beneficial it was that Christians began to see the Church as the People of God.[2] But already in the Initial Report, there is evidence of a *suspicion of the notion*. It appears, not in the summary of the fruits of the Council, but only in the section on abuses and errors, where it is used to illustrate superficial, incomplete, and even ideological readings of the Council's teaching on the Church. This alleged misuse of the term seems to account for its *near-disappearance from the Final Report*, an astounding development for a document which warns against partial and selective readings of the Council's texts.[3]

There is a second statement in the Final Report's comments on the mystery of the Church that indicates that another ecclesiological option is intended. It warns that 'we may not replace a false, one-sided and merely hierarchical vision of the Church with a new and also one-sided sociological concept of the Church'. In none of the previous Reports is this particular comment anticipated, but two earlier statements perhaps explain its origin. The Second Report said: 'Without this dimension of mystery, the Church would lose all significance for men, indeed it would lose its own identity and would be reduced to the level of other social institutions. It would have nothing to say, nothing to be.' The other comment occurred in the German language-group, which referred to 'the tendency to want to make the Church *ourselves* rather than to receive it from God. From the correct statement, "We *are* the Church", it is often mistakenly concluded, "we *make* the Church"'.[4]

If such statements underlie the remark of the Final Report, one can understand why it was said. The distinctiveness of the Church lies precisely in the *mystery of Christ celebrated and realized in it*; and in this sense, it is true that we 'receive' the Church from God. But it is also true that in many respects the Church is very much like other social bodies and even that there are senses in which we do ourselves build up the Church. Both of these features require a hierarchical and/or sociological approach to the Church, without which there is a great danger, unacknowledged in the Final Report, of an *equally incorrect and one-sided ecclesiology of mystery*. On this point, the Council's presentation in LG 8 was far more balanced.

The other ecclesiological notion stressed by the Final Report is that of '*communion*' which it describes as 'the central and fundamental idea in the Council's documents'. The notion has deep biblical and traditional roots; it refers primarily to 'communion with God through Christ and the Holy Spirit'; and it is realised through the Word of God and the sacraments. Here the Final Report *accurately reflects the Synod's discussion*, in which 'communion' was proposed by speakers of the most diverse backgrounds, interests and opinions. And, of course, it stresses a notion which was of primary importance in Vatican II itself.

But here too, it appears that 'communion' served *quite different purposes* when it was invoked at the Synod. The differences are discreetly revealed in the Final Report itself:

> For this reason, the ecclesiology of communion cannot be reduced to purely organisational questions or to questions simply about power. Nevertheless, the ecclesiology of communion is the foundation of Church order and especially of a correct relationship between unity and pluriformity in the Church.

Here the first sentence reflects an idea already stated in the Second Report: 'It was rightly stated in the hall that the men of today would not understand it if all that was discussed in this Synod was the distribution of powers in the Church.'[5] Since no one at the Synod appears to have wanted to reduce communion to the question of distribution of power, one is temped to wonder if the comment was not made in order to relativise that legitimate issue. If this is so, one can understand that the Final Report, in its desire to represent all views, immediately recalls that communion is the basis of Church order and of the relationship between unity and pluriformity.

For this second statement reflects a theme which is very prominent in some of the pre-synodal responses, was often urged in the first week's debate, and was strongly repeated in at least two of the language-groups: what Spanish language-group A called the '*horizontal dimension of communion*' and its implications for participation and co-responsibility. The Initial Report had frankly reported: 'What the Council taught about the Church as communion is sometimes neither understood nor put into practice.' And it illustrated this by the often noted controversies about 'the relationship between the universal Church and the particular churches, the understanding of collegiality with and under the Roman Pontiff and improving its practical implications, and the status of episcopal conferences'. It also noted the desire expressed in many pre-synodal reports for greater participation and co-responsibility and for improved communications, particularly in exchanges between the local churches and the Roman curia. Several of these issues were quite strongly stated also in the synodal interventions.

For these reasons, in his Second Report, Cardinal Danneels recommended that the language-groups study *communion in terms of the applicability of the principle of subsidarity*, the relationship between unity and pluriformity, the problem of enculturation, the understanding and practice of collegiality, and the role of episcopal conferences. But he also seemed to direct the discussion in a particular direction: 'Collegiality is a sacramentally grounded reality, and therefore the collegial spirit is broader than a merely juridical exercise of collegiality. Since it is a sacramental reality, a theology of collegiality cannot be reduced to a mere debate about consultative or deliberative power. This should be kept in mind in discussions about improving the synod of bishops.' Here again the appeal to collegial spirit and its sacramental basis has the effect of relativising the significance of debates about structure in the Church, when it could as justly be argued that the *questions arise precisely because the sacramental and collegial foundations require more appropriate structures and relationships*.

In any case by the Final Report, almost all of the serious questions raised about the concrete structural implications of ecclesial communion have either disappeared or been translated into questions of vague collegial 'spirit'. This will be evident if we review some of the particular issues.[6]

3. THE REALISATION OF ECCLESIAL COMMUNION

(a) *Unity and Diversity*. This was a major preoccupation in the reports from the churches where it was raised particularly as the question of the relationship between the universal Church and the local churches and involved the problem of enculturation as well as structural relationships within the Church. In the Initial Report, the Council's statement that 'the one and universal Church exists in and out of the particular churches' was described as 'one of the most important statements' in *Lumen Gentium* and was invoked as 'the basis for legitimate pluralism within the unity of the Church'. But little of the basic or specific issues remains in the Final Report which instead offers a redefinition of the very terms of the discussion:

> Here we have the true theological principle of variety and pluriformity in unity; but this pluriformity must be distinguished from mere pluralism. Since pluriformity is true richness and implies fullness, it is true catholicity; but a pluralism of mainly opposed positions leads to dissolution and destruction and to a loss of identity.

The reasons for this redefinition of the terms of the discussion are nowhere discussed; this semantic change, introduced in the Second Report, does not seem to have been requested by any speaker at the Synod.

(b) *Enculturation*. A reading of the responses from the churches will indicate how often reference was made to this theme and not only by churches in 'the Third World'. But it received only a very brief notice in the Initial Report. After it was often mentioned in the synod hall as a major challenge for the Church to confront, the Second Report treated it as part of the question of unity and pluriformity and offered a definition that was later taken over by the Final Report:

> Here we also have the theological principle for the problem of enculturation. Since the Church is a communion which joins diversity and unity, by its presence throughout the world it takes up whatever positive elements it finds in each culture. Yet enculturation is different from mere external adaptation, since it means the intimate transformation of authentic cultural values through their integration into Christianity and by rooting Christianity in the various human cultures.

In the Final Report, enculturation is given stronger support than in the earlier reports; but it *still appears as something which will affect the cultures more than the Church itself*, as perhaps is already implied by its being moved from the section on Church as communion to the one on the Church's mission in the world. There is no reference to the often-voiced request of the local churches for greater freedom of adaptation in order to meet the challenge of enculturation.[7]

(c) *Collegiality*. This section of the Final Report contents itself with a description of the sacramental foundation of collegiality, a distinction between collegial spirit (*affectus*) and collegial activity in the strict sense, and an insistence that the issue be posed correctly, not as a distinction between the Roman Pontiff and the bishops taken collectively, but between the *Roman Pontiff by himself and the Roman Pontiff along with the bishops*, a description borrowed from the famous *Nota praevia explicativa*. These remarks are followed by descriptions of collegiality in a broad sense:

> From this first collegiality, understood in the strict sense, one must distinguish the different partial realisations which are truly a sign and instrument of collegial spirit: the synod of bishops, episcopal conferences, the Roman curia, *ad limina* visits, etc. All of these realisations cannot be deduced directly from the theological principle of collegiality; they are, rather, governed by ecclesiastical law. Still these and other forms, such as the pastoral journeys of the Supreme Pontiff, are a very important service to the whole college of bishops along with the pope, as also for the individual bishops, whom the Holy Spirit has appointed to govern the Church of God (see Acts 20:28).

What is interesting here is not only the very selective references to the Council's discussion of collegiality, the effort theologically and ecclesially to deflate the various expressions of collegial spirit,[8] and the curious mixture of things considered to exemplify collegiality, but the *total absence of any reference to the many problems raised* in the responses of the churches, in the Initial Report, in the synodal interventions, and in the Second Report, about the *practical implementation of collegiality*. Here is the clearest indication that, in the Final Report, invocations of 'communion' and 'collegial spirit' have triumphed over *frank admission of serious problems of structure and relations in the Church today*.

(d) *Participation and Co-responsibility*. Here the Final Report begins with a *clear and strong statement*: 'Because the Church is a communion, there must be participation and co-responsibility at all of her levels', a claim which it then illustrates at all levels except the highest.

No such section can be found in the Second Report, but a need for it was clearly indicated in the Initial Report:

> The Church's structure as a communion would certainly be diminished if it were reduced only to hierarchical communion with the episcopal college and with the task of universal unity, that is, with the Petrine ministry. For in the Church communion between bishops and presbyters, between bishops and theologians, between priests

and laypeople, between men and women, between the poor and the rich, must be put into practice more and more and made to conform to a more perfect rule.

It is good that the Final Report returns to this emphasis, even though its statements do not go much beyond the hortatory.

(e) *The Synod of Bishops*. Here one must note the *complete absence from the Final Report of any reference to the synod itself*, except as an illustration of the *affectus collegialis*, despite the fact that several of the pre-synodal responses and oral interventions had raised questions about its procedures, questions to which Pope John Paul II himself refers in his concluding address.

The Extraordinary Assembly itself *reflected some of these problems*. The whole process was largely still governed by a *concern for secrecy* one hoped had by now been dissipated. The episcopal conferences were ordered not to publish their pre-synodal reports. The Initial and Second Reports of Cardinal Danneels were not released to the press. Most of the oral and written interventions during the first week and all of the reports from the language-groups were available only in the sketchiest of summaries. The expert advisers to the conferences were not permitted to attend the sessions. All this leaves the impression that the synod is conceived of as a kind of 'Privy Council' to the pope. There is very little evidence of it as an opportunity for that *mutual exchange* in which *Lumen Gentium* 13 had found the essence of the Church's catholicity.

A *second example is symbolic*. The instant that the members of the Synod decided to issue a 'Message' to the Church, they were told by the presidents who would write it. This was doubly surprising, for no synod-regulation requires this nomination, and no Synod member appears to have urged the right of the synod to choose who would write their own message.

Finally, there is a serious problem with the *constitution* of the *Circuli minores*. The principle by which Synod members were designated to the various groups is solely *linguistic*: they chose to join a Latin, English, German, French, Italian or Spanish language-group. (Where their numbers were too large, they were divided into two, by alphabetical order.)

This arrangement has both advantages and disadvantages. It can be very enlightening for bishops to see how a particular problem is perceived and dealt with in different churches; this can relativise one's own perceptions and provide a genuinely ecclesial correction, confirmation or challenge. On the other hand, it can also make it much more difficult for bishops to understand one another. Above all, it introduces an artificial and ecclesially marginal principle. Language, of course, is one basic component of a culture and, therefore, is part of the socio-cultural dimension of a local church. But it is certainly not the only one and in many areas it is not the most crucial one. Indeed, the languages in which, in many countries, the Church is seeking to enculturate the Gospel are not the European languages but the native languages of the people. This linguistic bias in favour of the languages of Europe is perhaps inevitable, but it should make one reflect that at the Synod the principle by which the *Circuli minores* are set up has so little to do with the linguistic, economic, social, political and cultural conditions in which local churches live and act. Politically, this also has the effect of hindering the formation of 'blocs', which perhaps is one of its purposes.

CONCLUSION

I have concentrated on the ecclesiological issues as these were raised at the Synod and have tried to indicate how well they are reflected in the Final Report. Some *observations* suggest themselves.

First, this Synod, as the last several before it, was an occasion on which the serious problems of *implementing the Council's ecclesiology* were again raised, discussed and displayed. The most serious ones are somewhat distinct but related: what one might call the 'cultural' and the 'structural' realisation of ecclesial communion in a genuinely and concretely catholic Church. The *cultural dimension* refers to the challenge to reconcile unity and plurality in the Church particularly after centuries of European cultural dominance within the Church itself. The slogan for this is 'enculturation', and we have seen that this challenge, vigorously argued both before and during the Synod, is very muted in the Final Report.

The *structural dimension* is related: how, particularly after centuries of Roman centralisation, to realise local churches, genuinely responsible for themselves even while in communion with the other churches. The questions entailed by this challenge were also raised, and with even greater vigour, both before and during the Synod. But they too were *poorly represented in the Final Report*, which even appears to want to bury them under a blanket of 'collegial spirit' or by appeals to an allegedly forgotten or neglected ecclesiology of mystery and communion.

This is the importance of the *question of the basic notion of the Church*. No one should regret it if the mystery of Christ's redemptive work, word and grace becomes more central both to the life of the Church and in ecclesiology. But it is a major ecclesiological mistake to *emphasise mystery to the neglect of other dimensions of the Church*, equally necessary to the life of the Church on its pilgrimage in history and equally emphasised by the Council. Similarly, the vertical dimension of communion with God is inescapably bound up with its horizontal dimension of communion among the churches. Where the latter is not considered to be an implication of the former or where its practical implications are not boldly and honestly addressed, people are likely to think either that the true dimensions of the communion of all in God, in Christ, and in the Spirit are not really taken seriously or that the appeal to 'communion' conceals other agendas.

The issues at stake here, both theoretical and practical, are very large indeed, which is why the Synod inspired so much attention and passion. The practical issues will take decades, if not centuries, to resolve, if indeed they can be resolved without tension at all. The theoretical issues remain those stated by the Council, whose description of the challenge to theologians is far more complete and balanced than that of the Final Report. *The Extraordinary Synod of 1985 resolved neither the theoretical nor the practical problems.* That challenge remains before us.

Notes

1. The fullest documentation on the Synod so far available is provided in *Le Synode extraordinaire* (Paris 1986), for which I provided the 'Introduction', which develops further the analysis given in this essay.

2. See the pre-synodal reports from England and Wales, the United States, and Brazil. At the Synod, 'mystery' was particularly promoted by bishops from Western Europe and the Roman curia, while 'People of God' was particularly stressed by Third World bishops.

3. Before the Synod, Cardinal Ratzinger twice repeated his long-standing critique of the notion 'People of God', see the third chapter of *The Ratzinger Report: An Exclusive Interview on the State of the Church* (San Francisco 1985) (Rapporto sulla fede [Milano 1985]), and his far more balanced essay 'L'ecclesiologia del Vaticano II' in *La Chiesa del Concilio: Studi e Contributi* (Milano 1985) pp. 9–24. See also the survey article by Giuseppe Colombo 'Il "popolo di Dio" e il "mistero" della Chiesa nell'ecclesiologia post-conciliare' *Teologia* 10 (1985) 97–169

4. Language very similar to this is also found in chapter 3 of Cardinal Ratzinger's interview. Just before the Synod met, the International Theological Commission issued a small book, *L'unique Eglise du Christ* (Paris 1985), on selected aspects of the ecclesiology of Vatican II. This includes an interesting chapter on 'L'Eglise comme "mystère" et "suject historique"', but this does not appear to have influenced the Final Report.

5. This appears to refer to Cardinal Ratzinger, who is reported to have said; 'The distribution of powers cannot be the central theme of the Synod.' A week earlier, at the Consistory of Cardinals, he had exhorted his colleagues not to give the impression 'that we, like the disciples in the Cenacle, are only discussing which of us is the greater, and this at the very time when the members of Christ are suffering and asking us for the bread of life.'

6. Since separate articles are devoted to episcopal conferences and to the principle of subsidiarity, I have omitted reference to them here.

7. Perhaps this is the place to note the curious attempts to re-define *aggiornamento.* The Final Report discusses it in the context of an emphasis on the Cross, which it

apparently believes has been neglected recently. 'From this paschal perspective, which affirms the unity of the cross and resurrection, the true and false meaning of so-called "aggiornamento" is discerned. It is not mere easy accommodation, which would lead to the secularisation of the Church. Nor is it an unmoveable closing in upon itself of the community of the faithful. It is, rather, missionary openness for the integral salvation of the world. Through it, all truly human values are not only accepted but vigorously defended: the dignity of the human person, basic human rights, peace, freedom from oppression, misery and injustice. But integral salvation is only obtained if these human realities, often deformed by sin, are purified and further raised by grace to familiarity with God through Jesus Christ in the Holy Spirit.'

A few things are odd about this description. First, no recorded discussion before or during the Synod suggests it as a definition of *aggiornamento*. Second, it appears in the discussion of the Church in the modern world, where it functions as part of the one-way description of the need for the Church to 'purify' values honoured by the world. Thirdly, it has completely lost the connotations it had in Pope John's use of it, which included the need for the Church to criticise and reform itself in the light of modern challenges. Of course, this latter emphasis is in considerable tension with the earlier statement that 'the Church is one and the same throughout all the Councils'.

8. At least the Final Report does not include the controversial paragraph of the book published by the International Theological Commission, which maintained that collegiality could be applied to institutions such as episcopal conferences 'only in an analogous, theologically improper sense' (see *L'unique Eglise du Christ*, p. 38).

Jean-Marie Tillard

Final Report of the Last Synod

ANYONE WHO has followed with interest the preparations for the last Synod, carefully analysed the preliminary studies, and assessed the reactions of various Christian circles to one or the other more effective documents, must find the final report a pleasure to read. One's first impression is favourable. A more analytical and exacting second reading prompts one to revise that spontaneous reaction, but only in order to elucidate and not to reject it. In spite of the very little time they had and especially the speed of their preparation (there were scarcely ten months between the Synod's announcement and its opening), the bishops of the whole world reaffirmed the essentials of Vatican II.

In this quick survey, and in the small space granted me, I do not intend to comment on the report (others have already done so, and it is pointless to repeat their work). Instead I shall scrutinise it in regard to its status as *a crucial stage in the 'reception' of the last council*. To be sure, the bishops would have needed more time for their text to express quite adequately what I would term the condition of the 'reception' of Vatican II, and it would have been necessary to have taken the pulse, as it were, of local churches more effectively.[1] In addition, many members of the Synod were not at Vatican II and their knowledge of the major intuitions of the council, and in particular of the deep motivation underlying one or the other formulation, would seem on occasion to have been rather fragmentary. Finally, the publication and exchange between churches of replies to the preparatory questionnaire would have allowed each bishops' conference to examine the experience of neighbouring churches, and thus to establish their judgment more soundly.[2] On the other hand, this situation has a positive aspect: it gives one an excellent notion of the Catholic bishops' habitual awareness of the council, twenty years after it was held.

1. VATICAN II 'CONFIRMED' IN ITS ENTIRETY—BUT RE-READ WITH NEW EYES

(a) Assimilation, yet re-reading

Talk of the 'reception' of a council, especially one which produced such a vast amount of documentation, necessarily means *assimilation of its content in accordance with the pace of ecclesial life*. Yet it is noteworthy that the final report of the 1985 Synod, two decades after the end of Vatican II, already indicates a *shift from, a re-reading of, some of its conspicuous points*. To be sure, there is neither denial nor rejection of any part of it, and, after re-reading the minutes of the discussions, I am convinced that the document's second paragraph is faithful when it states: 'The reason why this Synod was called was the celebration, verification, and promotion of the second Vatican council. We gratefully acknowledge that with divine assistance these effects have actually been felt. Unanimously we have celebrated the second Vatican council as a grace of God and as a gift of the Holy Spirit. It has afforded numerous spiritual fruits for the universal Church and for individual churches, as well as for people of our time. We have also assured ourselves unanimously and joyfully that the second Vatican council is a legitimate and valid expression and an interpretation of the deposit of faith as contained in Holy Scripture and in the living Tradition of the Church. Therefore we have decided to continue along the route marked out for us by the council. In full agreement we have acknowledged the necessity increasingly to promote the knowledge and application of the council, both in the letter and in the spirit. In this way new steps will be taken in the reception of the council: in, that is, its spiritual interiorisation and practical application.'[3]

It is evident, nevertheless, that viewpoints and therefore *readings often differ*.

(i) The re-appraisal of secular reality. The most telling sign of this difference is to be found in the *judgment made of secular reality*. As against their predecessors' optimistic assessment, the bishops of 1985 take a realistic view of actuality. Moreover they opine: 'The short period between us and the end of the council is marked historically by instances of accelerated change. Accordingly, at some points the signs of our times do not coincide exactly with those which comprised the conciliar context (II. A,1); and, again: 'Nevertheless we see that the signs of the present time differ to some extent from those of the period of the council, for trials and tribulations have grown worse. Today, indeed, throughout the world we are witnessing an increase of hunger, oppression, injustice and war, and more torture, terrorism and other forms of violence of all kinds. We are forced to reflect theologically in a new and deeper

way if we are to interpret these signs in the light of the Gospel' (II. D, 1). In this context, the report firmly stresses the danger of secularism (different to secularisation) and of a form of immanentism (I. 4; II. A, 1): that is, of a rejection of transcendence conducing to 'a new idolatry, to the slavery of ideologies, to a life shackled by the reductive and often oppressive structures of this world' (II. A, 1). The report also mentions the 'manifestations in our time too of the activity of the prince of this world and of the mystery of iniquity' (I. 4). The only positive sign stressed is the tendency to return to the sacred (II. A, 1).

This is no longer the exact overall emphasis of *Gaudium et Spes*. Moreover, though we read that it is necessary to 'exclude any immobile turning in of the community of the faithful on itself' just as much as that 'mere adaptation which might lead to the secularisation of the Church' (II. D, 3), there is no longer any firm encouragement of cooperation with all men and women of good will. The call for prudence rather obscures that openness.

(ii) Return to Redemption through the Cross. On studying the sections of the report which have to do with the question of relations between Church and world, one becomes convinced that the Church's mission is primarily to be understood as an identification with the ever-present struggle of Jesus Christ stretched out on the Cross. In fact it is revealing that after having mentioned the growth of trials and tribulations in our societies, a direct connection is made: 'It appears that in present difficulties God wishes to instruct us more deeply about the value, importance and central position of the cross of Jesus Christ. The relation between human history and salvation history has to be explained in the light of the Easter mystery. Of course, the theology of the cross in no way excludes the theology of creation and incarnation, but clearly presupposes it. When we Christians talk of the cross, we ought not to be described as pessimists, for we base our discourse on the realism of Christian hope.'

This paragraph (II. D, 2), in which the statement 'Of course, the theology of the cross in no way excludes the theology of creation and incarnation, but clearly presupposes it' did not appear in the first versions, *also contrasts with the tone of Gaudium et Spes.*

In fact Vatican II, which in no way questioned the importance of the Cross, preferred to consider Christians in their incarnate commitment to a continuously evolving creation, that human beings were properly called to bring to its due conclusion. It stressed the positive values which were always present in our world in spite of the forces of evil. Even though one must admit that Vatican II often relied on a notion of progress which was too strongly influenced by Enlightenment ideas, one must acknowledge the fact that its inspiration was drawn primarily from a traditional faith in Christ as Lord of creation and history, and from the biblical notion of 'the image of God'. The Synod, which was to return to the Cross in its final suggestions (II. D, 7), preferred once again to centre mission on the Redemption.

It then becomes clear why, in talking (at far too short a length) of human promotion, in a paragraph which also contains a splendid statement about the 'preferential option for the poor' (II. D, 6), the report emphasises commitment against various forms of alienation more than co-operation with vital forces constituting humanity.

(iii) The Church as a witness to Christ crucified rather than to itself. This stress on the Cross leads to a remark, inserted in an exposition regarding 'the mystery of God through Jesus Christ in the Holy Spirit', before a major statement about the sacramentality of the Church (II. A, 2). It says: 'The Church becomes more credible if it talks less about itself, increasingly preaches Christ crucified and testifies through its own life.' Here again there is a perceptible shift from Vatican II. If the statement was a slightly sarcastic judgment of the efforts made in the Church in respect of what the council called 'its permanent reformation', it would be most unhappy; and, as we know, some people have taken it in this way.[4] In fact it was in terms of its loyalty to Jesus Christ, and in order to be a sacrament more open to 'mystery', that the Church at Vatican II was concerned with itself, and its own structures and problems. Whatever aspect of its own self the Church presents to the world forms part of its preaching of Christ, dead and risen.

(b) Reweighting various approaches at Vatican II

Another register is apparent when (again without any denial of anything at all) the final report alters the balance of the approaches of Vatican II. This time we have to do with a consideration of the very nature of the Church.

(i) Displacement of the accent on the Church as People of God. Everything goes to show that the vision of the Church as the People of God no longer receives the privileged treatment which was indicated by its position in the structure of *Lumen Gentium*, even though when the descriptions of the council recur it is to the fore, and even though we find a repeated assertion that the Church is 'a messianic people on its pilgrim way on earth' (II. A, 3; C, 2). No time is lost in condemning a unilateral sociological idea (*ibid*) which many people would treat as the result of a poor understanding of this notion. In his synthesis of answers to the preparatory questionnaire, Cardinal Danneels had selected as the main negative note the fact that 'in particular the idea of the Church as the People of God is defined ideologically and separated from other complementary ideas mentioned in the conciliar texts—hence the inappropri-

ate contrast between the 'People of God' and the 'hierarchical Church'.[5] This fear of democratism leads to a very considerable degree of discretion about the concept under discussion.

A result of this discretion is the absence—even from the paragraphs on communion, unity and pluriformity—of *any reference to the absolute equality of all baptised persons*, to their common dignity, and to their common responsibility, *which grounds and sums up the differences between functions and charisms*. The short statement about the 'new experience of us all being the Church', with a brief reference to the 'new kind of cooperation between laity and clergy' and to the spirit of availability of the laity, does not express as strongly as Vatican II the dogmatic profundity of this community of belonging and destiny (II.B,6). In shifting the emphasis which Vatican II placed on the idea of the People of God, one has also happened on the implications of that emphasis.

(ii) The sense of the Church as mystery. A privileged status is accorded the 'dimension of the divine or of mystery' which is constitutive of the Church, by making it the key to true knowledge of the Church (II. A, 2–3). The text is, to be sure, not sufficiently explicit to allow us to decide whether to think above all on the lines of the connection between the Church and the eternal plan of the Saviour God, fulfilled and revealed in Jesus Christ—the *mysterion* in the sense of Paul and Colossians and Ephesians—and contained in 'the good and joyful news of the choice, mercy and charity of God as manifest in the history of salvation and, in the fulness of time, culminating in Jesus Christ' (II. A, 2) or on the lines of emphasising the 'sacramental' status of the Church as a 'sign and means of communion with God and of communion and reconciliation among human beings'.[6]

Lumen Gentium opened with a long chapter on this subject. But I think I am correct in supposing that the final report of the Synod—which talks at length of the universal vocation to holiness (II. A, 4)—sees this relation to 'mystery' more in that aspect which is gratifying to the Church itself 'anticipating the new creature in it' (II. A, 3) than in the aspect of epiphany, of manifestation to the world. To be sure, it begins with a presentation of mission, 'salvation to be offered and communicated to human beings through the working of the Holy Spirit', announcement and message (II. A, 2). But it soon moves to a statement on the 'Church which contains sinners in its bosom and is both holy and called constantly to self-purification, which, among the persecutions of the world and the consolations of God, is always on its way to the Kingdom', so effectively that 'always present' in it 'are the mystery of the Cross and the mystery of the Resurrection' (II. A, 3). The constitution on the Church, which is referred to explicitly, sounded different. The few lines which the report summarises came at the end of a superb long evocation of the

Church's mission to the impoverished. We must remember this key passage, which risks falling into oblivion, and which follows directly on the statement on *subsistit in:*

'Just as Christ carried out the work of redemption in poverty and oppression, so the Church is called to follow the same path if it is to communicate the fruits of salvation to men. Christ Jesus, "though he was by nature God . . . emptied himself, taking the nature of a slave" (Phil. 2:6), and "being rich, became poor" (2 Cor. 8:9) for our sake. Likewise, the Church, although it needs human resources to carry out its mission, is not set up to seek earthly glory, but to proclaim, and this by its own example, humility and self-denial. Christ was sent by the Father to "bring good news to the poor . . . to heal the contrite of heart" (Luke 4:18), "to seek and to save what was lost" (Luke 19:10).

Similarly, the Church encompasses with its love all those who are afflicted by human misery and it recognises in those who are poor and who suffer, the image of its poor and suffering founder. It does all in its power to relieve their need and in them it strives to serve Christ. Christ, "holy, innocent and undefiled" (Heb. 7:26) knew nothing of sin (2 Cor. 5:21), but came only to expiate the sins of the people (see Heb. 2:17). The Church, however, clasping sinners to its bosom, at once holy and always in need of purification, follows constantly the path of penance and renewal.

'The Church, "like a stranger in a foreign land, presses forward amid the persecutions of the world and the consolations of God", announcing the cross and death of the Lord until he comes (see 1 Cor. 11:26). But by the power of the risen Lord it is given strength to overcome, in patience and in love, its sorrows and its difficulties, both those that are from within and those that are from without, so that it may reveal in the world, faithfully, however darkly, the mystery of its Lord until, in the consummation, it shall be manifested in full light.' (*Lumen Gentium* 8).

2. A CHURCH CENTRED MORE ON ITSELF AND ON THE VALUES OF INWARDNESS

(a) The continuing momentum of the opening up of the Church

An analysis of the final report carried out in the light of the documented replies to the questionnaire and of the internal Synod discussions, leads to what I beleve is a clear conclusion. The main thrust of the report is still that of the *opening up effected at Vatican II.* The far too pessimistic expectations of some linguistic groups were not wholly averted—they reappeared often, especially in the form of warnings and cautions—but they were at least inserted in more positive and less defeatist perspectives. Yet the document as a whole is strongly marked by a tendency to centre on the Church *in itself*, confronting its own problems; the influence *within it* of pernicious forces originating without and threatening to damage its loyalty to the Gospel; the effect *in it* of certain 'incomplete and selective readings of the Council'; the need *within it* for a more passionate search for sanctity; the repercussions *in it* of the drama of our age as evident especially in a secularisation hardly discerned for what it is and verging on secularism; and signs which give cause to suspect the presence *in it* of the wrong kind of pluralism contrasting quite with a healthy pluriformity (II. C, 2).[7]

Here too the emphasis is no longer that of Vatican II, disposed rather to take the risks associated with 'dialogue', cooperation, welcoming questions, and 'sympathy' (in the etymological sense) with all men and women who try to release humankind from harsh suffering. It is significant, for instance, that the declaration *Dignitatis humanae* on religious freedom is not referred to, especially when there is mention of 'the dignity of the human person, the basic rights of man, peace, freedom from oppression, impoverishment and injustice' (II. D, 3). Of course (and I repeat the point to make sure that it is grasped), it is a matter of *differing emphases and never of a rejection of what was worked out at Vatican II*. But this difference of emphasis shows how the Catholic bishops intuitively (or implicitly) believe that, in the great task of evangelisation entrusted to the Church (a theme on which the Synod spent some time), the moment has surely come for, so to speak, a diastolic effort by which vital forces can be brought to the heart for renewal.

(b) The Summons to inwardness

This diastolic movement explains the constant recurrence in the report of a *passionate evangelical summons to inwardness*. It is to be found elsewhere, even in the definition of dialogue: 'True dialogue leads the human individual to open up and to communicate his or her inwardness to the partner in dialogue' (II. D, 5). It is everywhere. In regard to the evangelisation of non-believers it is said that 'it presupposes the self-evangelisation of the baptised, and hence also of deacons, priests and bishops' (II. B, 2). In respect of the participation of the faithful in the liturgy, it is stated that 'it consists not only in an outward activity but much more in inward and spiritual participation' (II. B, 1).

In regard to *aggiornamento* we learn that it is true 'if human reality is purified and, ultimately, raised through grace to closeness to God, through Jesus Christ, in the Holy Spirit' (II. D, 3), which notion is applied to enculturation (II. D, 4). Its effect on a conception of *koinonia*—communion— is evident, and stress is laid on the idea that 'it is a matter basically of communion with God through Jesus Christ, in the Holy Spirit' (II. C, 1). This inwardness also marks a presentation of collegiality which brings out 'the collegial spirit, the essence of cooperation between bishops on the regional, national or international level' (II. D, 4). Ecumenical dialogue itself is described as 'depending in a special way on mutual prayer' (II. C, 7). These are all acceptable reminders.

Something which perhaps seems a trifle odd at this point is a certain reticence which contrasts with one of the main preoccupations of the bishops at Vatican II. To begin with, sanctification here would seem to be identified so surely with what I have called inwardness, that there is now no mention whatsoever of the *sanctifying effect of apostolic commitment* as such where it is experienced in full communion with Jesus Christ. A lacuna indeed, but one which we should not unjustly ascribe to a supposedly concealed intention. But lacunae often reveal states of mind.

While we are on the subject of sanctification, it should be noted that the few allusions to the Holy Spirit, almost all of which occur in the sections emanating from the same source, do not succeed in hiding the survival of a *Christomonism* which is typical of the West even though post-conciliar theology has often reacted against it. Loyalty to the great patristic tradition is not shown by scattering about a few sentences referring to the Holy Spirit. It is astonishing that in the paragraph on the 'mystery of the Church' the Holy Spirit is not mentioned apart from a list of church figures (II. A, 3), and that the 'universal vocation to holiness' is discussed without any reference to him (II. A, 4). Surely that is why this very unsatisfactory part of the document has such a highly moralising style.

(c) A full presentation of the Church as Communion

Even though this tendency of the Church to turn in on itself and its worries about the loyalty of Christians to their life of grace lead to some shifts from the emphases of Vatican II, they also tend to stress firmly one of the main reaffirmations of the council—perhaps one which gave ecclesial life of the last two decades its most valuable support. The final report spends time on a full presentation of the 'Church as communion'. This *koinonia*-communion, which is consistently referred to in the main conciliar documents, is conceived here in terms both *of its essence and of its application in the structuring and life of the Church*. Though the tone of the entire report seems to intend a special stress on the Church-as-mystery, in the end these superb pages on communion will remain the most important to result from this Synod's labours. They do indeed represent 'verification' and 'promotion' of Vatican II and I consider them a *major advance in its 'reception'*.

(i) This idea as a major fruit of the Synod. The considerable attention which

the report pays to this point (in which the report of the International Theological Commission showed some interest, especially in the perspective of 'hierarchically ordered' and organised 'social communion', preferring otherwise to speak of 'community';[8] and about which Cardinal Danneels' synthesis was quite laconic)[9] is certainly due to discussions within the Synod. The extremely interesting text produced by the Bishops' Conference of England and Wales (10 and 11 July 1985), and Cardinal Hume's theologically-grounded intervention relying on an ecumenical experience of twenty years of dialogue, were influential. When Cardinal Hume explained why the concept of *koinonia*-communion takes us to the very essence of the mystery which is the Church[10], he gave dogmatic shape to an intuition woven into the documents of Vatican II, worked on in post-conciliar life, and verified in ecumenical dialogues. Taken up by one of the English-speaking groups at the Synod—17 out of 21 of its members came from the Third World—this great vision passed into the final text and *became in fact its key idea*.[11]

(ii) The Report's definition of Communion. The report's definition of communion is important: 'What does this complex word 'communion' mean? It is basically a matter of communion with God, through Jesus Christ, in the Holy Spirit. This communion is effected in the Word of God and in the sacraments. Baptism is the gate and foundation of the communion of the Church. The Eucharist is the source and summit of all Christian lives (see LG 11). Communion with the eucharistic Body of Christ means and produces, or constructs, the intimate communion of all the faithful in the Body of Christ, which is the Church (see 1 Cor. 10:16). Hence the ecclesiology of communion cannot be reduced to mere questions of organisation or to problems which have to do only with mere powers. The ecclesiology of communion is also the foundation of order in the Church, and in particular of a proper relationship between unity and pluriformity in the Church' (II. C, 1).

Here we see the effect of what ecumenical discussions, especially with the Eastern churches and those of the Anglican communion, slowly worked out and laid down on the basis both of central Tradition and the emphases of Vatican II.

(iii) The balanced possession of a now common outlook about collegiality. The paragraphs on collegiality, participation, coresponsibility and 'ecumenical communion' merely express what has become the common outlook in the Catholic Church, but the balanced and calm way in which relations between the Bishop of Rome (unfortunately he is still referred to as the Roman Pontiff), the other bishops, and all local churches are considered in this section of the report is noteworthy. Everything is seen in a perspective of solidarity, service, and cohesion in unity. What one of my Orthodox friends described as 'the Catholic obsession with papal power' is wholly absent. Here

one can feel the effect of a new dynamism looking for an osmosis between the life which passes from the local churches to the church of Rome and that extending from the church of Rome to other local churches.

(iv) Pluriformity in unity. Whatever the somewhat rabbinical distinction between pluralism and pluriformity may mean, the few lines on 'variety and pluriformity in unity' and on pluriformity, 'true riches' which 'bring fulness with them' and 'are themselves a true form of catholicity' (II. C, 2) are replete with implications. Undoubtedly enculturation projects will often look to this section for support (even now see *ibid.*, II. D, 4), and it will be consulted for help in the ecumenical quest for *a form of communion which does not mean one group absorbing another.* But we must acknowledge here—and this too means a lot—a sign of recognition of new churches as equally entitled members of the Catholic communion, and a token of a serious attitude to their individual riches. They are no longer mere 'dependent churches'. Here again the vision of Vatican II has been consolidated.

3. AN EPISCOPAL BODY THAT WANTS TO BREAK THROUGH DEAD-ENDS

(a) Surmounting obstacles to a continuing life

In the mosaic of fragments taken from various perspectives, and often from the results of discussions by linguistic groups of quite different outlooks, which comprises the final Synod report, there are certain pieces which evince a firm desire to advance and to surmount obstacles which threaten continuing life. Their true meaning is apparent only when they are located in the document as a whole, where they appear as *breaches into the future.*

(i) Scattered allusions to delicate topics. It is a matter primarily of a few allusions to situations which, in certain ecclesiastical settings, would be disapproved of and sometimes even criticised as giving rise to conflict. The most typical is probably the allusion to '*basic Church communities*', about which the Synod had something to say, prompted perhaps in this by Paul VI's attitude in *Evangelii nuntiandi*: 'Since the Church is communion, if they live truly in the unity of the Church the new "basic Church communities" are an authentic expression of communion and a means of building a more profound communion. Therefore they constitute a theme of great hope for the life of the Church (see EN 58)' (II. C, 6).

How could anyone say that 'it was mistaken to think that the bishops would support the *Latin American experiments*'? There was certainly a favourable judgment of one of the Church contexts in which, especially in Latin America, human desires for liberation and attachment to the faith are joined in a unique quest for salvation.

The same spirit is apparent in the long paragraph entitled '*preferential option for the poor and human promotion*' (II. D, 6). Extended to the dimensions of all forms of impoverishment—'lack of freedom, and spiritual possessions', deprivation of 'basic and inalienable rights of the human individual', attaching to life 'from the start'—this text reflects the often tragic experience of the churches of the poor, especially in Latin America. Then the following lines offer their full import: 'The Synod expresses its communion with those brothers and sisters suffering persecution because of their faith or in order to promote justice, and its prayers rise to God on their behalf.

The saving mission of the Church in regard to the world must be seen as integral. Though it is spiritual, the mission of the Church implies the promotion of human beings in the temporal domain as well. Therefore the Church's mission cannot be reduced to a monism in any sense of the word. Clearly, this mission implies a clear distinction but not a separation between natural aspects and those of grace. This duality is not a dualism. And so we have to avoid and advance beyond false and useless oppositions: that, for instance, between spiritual mission and being in the world's service.'[12]

(ii) An enhanced commitment to ecumenism. In a quite different context, even though shortly before the Synod the *ecumenical commitment of the Catholic Church* seemed on the point of compromise[13], voices were heard in its defence in the full session of the synod.[14] English-speaking working groups had even made it a major priority. The final report synthesizes this instance of ecumenical sympathy in a few sentences. It sees it as an option of the Catholic Church. On the one hand, it reaffirms the fact that the Church has an 'ecumenical responsibility' and that 'ecumenism is deeply and indelibly writ large in its consciousness' (II. CC, 7). On the other hand, on two occasions, it affirms that there is a communion with 'the non-Catholic churches and communities', 'even though it is still incomplete'. Though separated, they are in communion. And this belonging to a communion already connects them, in spite of the incomplete realisation of that communion, to the very essence of the Church if it is true that 'the Church is communion' (II. C, 6).

Therefore it is clear that the Catholic bishops have indeed 'received' Vatican II, and that they have breathed a new enthusiasm won from the practice of the last twenty years into this process of reception, the result is a treatment which brings out the loyalty of the Catholic Church to its very vocation as Church. It had been one of the main choices of Vatican II.

Outstanding Problems

I have already stressed the simplicity and moderation with which the final report tackles the delicate question of relations between the Bishop of Rome and the other bishops, and the church of Rome and other local churches. Two problems which have been suspended since the end of the council nevertheless still preoccupy the bishops and their churches. The Synod has opted for an open solution in this regard.

(i) The Scope of local initiative—subsidiarity. The first of these problems is the margin of freedom and initiative which is allowed each local church without any questioning of communion with the Catholic Church as a whole. At their Jakarta meeting from 3 to 13 November 1985, the Indonesian bishops expressed their ill-ease by asking the Synod to look at the difficulties caused by too great a degree of Roman centralisation.[15] At the Synod not only the Eastern bishops but bishops from Africa, Asia, the Caribbean and Scandinavia[16] expressed themselves similarly. The key to the question was, it would seem, to call in the *idea of subsidiarity.* Whereas one of the French-speaking groups came out against subsidiarity, seeing it as an obstacle to genuine collegiality, the final report asks that *this concept should be examined to see* 'to what extent and in what sense it could or should be applied (II. C, 8). Clearly the problem has been acknowledged and a solution is duly being sought for.

(ii) Episcopal Conferences. Of course there was a much thornier question— *episcopal conferences.* Powerful voices relayed with the help of the mass media had raised the question of their ecclesiological status, sometimes even over-emphasising the negative aspects. The *International Theological Commission* had made a quite decisive statement which had taken aback the whole theological world. After a very long examination the Commission declared that it was 'strictly speaking impossible to assign the qualification "collegial" to bishops' conferences and their continental groupings' and that the use of the term to qualify their activity was 'theologically impermissible'.[17] But, as a note from the Canadian bishops said, surely this very radical conclusion did not take into account the authority in the past of certain regional synods in communion with the Roman see. At the Synod one of the French-speaking groups took a sceptical attitude to this question, whereas other interventions asked that the role and authority of episcopal conferences should be taken absolutely seriously.

Once again the final report *opts for openness.* It stresses the necessity of bishops' conferences (II. C, 5) and above all asks that the quest should continue, since the negative outlook is not necessarily the right one: 'Since episcopal conferences are especially useful, even necessary, in the present pastoral work of the Church, an examination of their theological "status" is desirable, especially so that the question of their doctrinal authority may be more precisely and deeply explained, taking into account the contents of the conciliar decree *Christus dominus* 38 and the Code of Canon Law, can. 447 and 753' (II. C, 8).

The report omits, however, to say exactly who should pursue this quest, and what body is to be responsible for the associated decisions.

Faced with two tendencies, one more negative in regard to the effects of the council, the other more optimistic and more impatient to advance still further, the final Synod report—with a text that reveals the tensions between these two trends—shows the state of mind of the Catholic bishops twenty years after Vatican II. *The council has been 'received' but already life demands a reading of it which takes into account the experiences of those two decades.* And the Spirit of *communion,* in spite of everything, is opening up the way ahead, even though old spectres make occasional disquieting appearances.

Translated by J.G. Cumming

Notes

1. As emphasised by Mgr Hubert's intervention.
2. This is clear from the effects of the English bishops' text.
3. From the translation published with documentation in *La documentation catholique* (hereinafter referred to as DC), 83 (1986) No. 1909.
4. As early as 1.4 the report says: 'Perhaps we have laid ourselves open to criticism with too much talk of renewal of external structures of the Church and too little mention of God and Christ.'
5. See DC 83 (1986) 33.
6. There is a leap from one concept of mystery to another: 'mystery of God and human mystery' (II. A, 2), 'mystery of Christ and of the Church' (II. AA, 3), 'Church, mystery in Christ' (II. A, 4). These expressions do not have the same meaning as *mysterium* when synonymous with *sacramentum.* Compare the report of the International Theological Commission, *ibid.,* 73.
7. The novel distinction between pluralism ('juxtaposition of fundamentally opposed positions') and pluriformity is puzzling.
8. See DC 83 (1986) 66.
9. See *ibid.,* 33.
10. The original text of this intervention appeared in *The Tablet* (17 December 1985) 1297.
11. In the same way that *Lumen Gentium* was called 'a Belgian document', we may say that the final report of the Synod in this regard is an 'English document'.
12. But the Spanish-speaking group did not spend time on the theology of basic communities or on the preferential option for the poor; and in the discussion the Latin American churches appeared to be divided on these points.
13. Even if only by virtue of the status which was to be assigned to the Secretariat for Unity.
14. Thus Cardinals Hume and O'Fiaich, and Archbishop Carter (from Kingston, Jamaica).

15. See *The Tablet* (30 November 1985) 1272. The report of the Bishops of England and Wales showed the same tendency.

16. Archbishops Hurley, Carter, and Gran (Oslo).

17. See DC 83 (1986) 65.

Aloísio Lorscheider

The Extraordinary Synod in the Light of Vatican II Twenty Years Later

1. THE OBJECTIVES OF THE SYNOD

THE EXTRAORDINARY Synod was intended to be a commemoration, an exchange and an act of prophecy.

As a *commemoration*, according to the announcement by the Holy Father John Paul II, it was to revive the extraordinary atmosphere of ecclesial communion which characterised Vatican II in the reciprocal sharing of the sufferings and joys, the struggles and hopes of the body of Christ in the different regions of the world.

As an *exchange*, its purpose was to make better known and deepen experiences and information about the application of the Council at the level both of the universal Church and of particular churches.

As *prophecy*, its aim was to encourage the further elaboration and the constant insertion of Vatican II in the life of the Church, in response also to the new demands of the new 'signs of the times'.

In short, the Synod was to recall, bear witness to and reaffirm what Vatican II was and what it sought to be. Twenty years might have helped us to understand better the purpose of divine providence in the Council. Secondly, an examination of the *new signs of the times* would help to situate it in the next phase of the world's history.

2. CARRYING OUT THE OBJECTIVES

The great difficulty in attaining the objectives fixed was the short duration of the Synod (24 November—8 December, which, discounting Sundays, the Immaculate Conception and Saturday afternoons, left a mere 11 days for real work) and the lack of time for adequate preparation. The *doctrinal and pastoral agendas were long*. They consisted not only of the 20 years of implementation of Vatican II, but also, and much more important, of the relevance of Vatican II today, its effects on the Church and the world, as a historical fact active in the present. It was unclear which aspect should be stressed, celebration, evaluation or projection into the future.

As it turned out, full justice was done to the *celebratory aspect*. An important contribution to this was the 'Historical Report' by Cardinal Gabriel Maria Garrone. Garrone stressed the role of the Council as a 'magnificent spiritual and ecclesial experience'. The hearts and souls of the Council fathers experienced realities which went beyond the sensible and reached the transcendent. There had been no lack of difficulties: the initial difficulty when it was not clear what the purpose of the Council was, the problem of the method to be followed in the work of the Council, and the inherent difficulties of the issues; nonetheless, the difficulties had not quenched the joy rooted in faith and nourished by charity. The joy had been much greater than the difficulties.

The Council left the Catholic bishops feeling a keen need for closer communion with each other, especially in relation to action. Collegiality became the characteristic feature of this Council, making ecclesiology the unifying centre of all Vatican II's work.

The *exchange of information* about the application of Vatican II in the Church spread around the world was also done well. We found that the Council had been well received by the faithful, particularly the liturgical renewal, the vast spread of the word of God, the renewed sense among the laity of belonging to the Church, the renewal of religious life, the awakening of an ecumenical spirit among the faithful, the sense of the Church's missionary duty and task and the sense of the Church's missionary nature, the experience of collegiality at all levels, the sense of the basic rights of the human person, and the sharpened social sense of the faithful. As regards the Church in itself, negative phenomena were also found, though these cannot be attributed to Vatican II itself, but rather to an incorrect or hasty interpretation of the council: *Post concilium, non necessarie ergo propter concilium*. One important set of questions which emerged after Vatican II centred on the relationship between the universal Church and the particular churches. Above all the question was what to do to make the collegial aspect of the Church better understood and more fully practised. What was the theological status of episcopal conferences?

As regards the relationship of the *Church to the world* (*Ecclesia ad extra*, *ecclesia in mundo huius temporis*, according to the decree *Gaudium et Spes*) it was noted that the conditions of today are very different from those of 20 years ago. The rich countries are suffering the effects of secularism, atheism, practical materialism and indifferentism. More or less the whole world is suffering from a grave spiritual crisis, in particular as regards moral principles and the hierarchy of values. In the countries of the Third World poverty, indeed destitution, has increased.

The persecutions and attacks the Church suffers in various places were remembered, how in some areas it is unjustly reduced to silence. Exposed to suffering and martyrdom, it is prevented from proclaiming the Gospel.

Nor can we forget the great problems of peace and war, the great scientific inventions, particularly in biogenetics. The place of women in society and in the Church is becoming more and more important.

In what state are the rights to truth and religious freedom? What is the relationship between faith and politics?

The aspect of *projecting Vatican II into the immediate future* was inadequately dealt with. Lack of time made any serious thinking impossible. The Synod ended by stressing various themes: the importance of the theology of the cross and the paschal mystery in the Church's preaching, in the sacraments and in the life of the Church in our time, the need to take further the preferential option for the poor, the theology and practice of enculturation and the dialogue with non-Christian religions and non-believers, the Church's social teaching on human development in constantly changing situations.

3. THE ATMOSPHERE OF THIS SYNOD AND ITS PRINCIPAL DECISION

In order to convey the atmosphere of this Extraordinary Synod I can do no better than summarise here the *first speech of Cardinal Juan Landázuri Ricketts*, archbishop of Lima (Peru).

Cardinal Landázuri began by saying that the fruits of the Council were undeniable. It was a new Pentecost. The Church had the opportunity to get to know itself better, began an internal renewal and started to listen to the world. The Council made us enter human history; it taught us to pay attention to the poor. The cardinal then recalled the two great general assemblies of the Latin American bishops, in Medellín (1968) and Puebla (1979). The Church, he said, now enjoyed greater credibility among ordinary people. The people of God wanted to take part in the life of the Church. Communion with the Vicar of Christ had been deepened. Episcopal conferences had become valid pastoral instruments. Lay people were acquiring a greater sense of their responsibility in the plan of salvation.

On the other hand, there was also ignorance about Vatican II. Some people wanted greater certainty, while others would be quite happy for everything to start again afresh. Because of some misinterpretations there was fear and pessimism. None of this, however, should turn us into prophets of doom, something Pope John XXIII warned us against long ago.

In an atmosphere of reasoned optimism and great joy and hope, the Synod fathers, *una cum Petro et sub Petro*, said that Vatican II is the Magna Carta for us today and for the future, the sign that the Church, as it journeys towards the third millennium, nourished by the Word of God, will celebrate the mysteries of Christ for the salvation of the world.

4. SOME PERSONAL OBSERVATIONS

I feel that the concerns of some Synod fathers very clearly influenced this extraordinary Synod, and an understanding of them helps to situate it better.

4.1 The main concern was with the *internal* problems of the Church, beginning with the concept of the Church itself.

4.2 The desire to stress the Church as mystery, and so the tendency to give priority to the image of the body of Christ and the temple of the holy Spirit, and not so much that of the *people of God*, was very evident. There was a fear in some quarters, hinted at rather than openly expressed, that the image of the 'people of God' had been misunderstood, and had given rise to a view of the Church which was 'sociological' rather than 'theological', creating the danger of a degeneration into a merely 'democratic' view of the Church. There was great stress on the idea of communion, much less on that of participation.

4.3 Also in this connection, there was some criticism of the principle of *subsidiarity*, which was felt by some to be valid in sociology but not in ecclesiology.

4.4 There were also signs on various occasions of a worry which had already been expressed at Vatican II, that collegiality could in some way affect papal primacy. This explains the stress on the pope in himself and the pope acting with the bishops. These formulations were not completed by any further consideration of how the pope should exercise this power with the bishops, given the present situation of the world and the enormous possibilities of communication. To put it more clearly, should the pope normally act alone or collegially? The nature of the Synod of bishops could perhaps be further defined in this context.

4.5 Great stress was also laid by some fathers on the *unitas fidei*, and a concern with doctrine made itself felt on a number of occasions. It was not clear whether the aim was to stress the *unitas fidei sic et simpliciter*, putting all the emphasis on the correct formulation of doctrine, or whether the desire was to stress the *unitas fidei vivida*. Which is more important, unity in formulations of the faith or unity in the way the faith is lived? I think this question should be given greater attention, and I feel that it could have great importance in ecumenism.

4.6 A piece of new terminology made its appearance at this Synod which I failed to understand. A distinction was made between 'pluralism' and 'pluriformity'. The term 'pluralism' was taken in a negative sense, as a defence of inherently opposed positions, leading to a weakening, destruction and loss of identity, while the term 'pluriformity' was taken in a positive sense as indicating the true wealth included in plenitude.

4.7 Considering this Synod as a whole, I was left with the impression that the main problem was that of *desacralisation or secularism*, which could be defined as an autonomistic vision of human beings and the world which leaves out the dimension of mystery, forgets it or even ignores it. There was almost a refrain: 'Back to the sacred!'

Here the *emergence and spread of the sects* emerged as a criticism of our own pastoral practice. The question was whether we are sufficiently aware of the spiritual hunger and thirst of people today, especially young people, and whether in our pastoral work we are doing enough to meet it.

The efforts made to draw attention to *institutionalised injustice and the growing phenomenon of domination* in the modern world were fruitless. They appeared in the final report and in the message the Synod addressed to the world as a change in the signs of the times. The *preferential option for the poor* as such appeared in very muted form, and without the necessary urgency. There was far from being any real interest in a Church of the poor or a poor Church, a Church in which the poor have status and a voice and a Church of the first beatitude. The idea that the Church should change its position in society has still made very little headway at the level of the universal Church. Care was even taken to avoid the word 'liberation', which appears only once in the final report. The expression 'integral salvation' was preferred. For my part I do not see much difference between integral liberation in Jesus Christ and integral salvation in Jesus Christ.

Translated by Francis McDonagh

PART III

The Consequences of the Synod

Elias Zoghby

The Universal Catechism Proposed by the Extraordinary Synod of Bishops, Considered from a Cultural and Pastoral Viewpoint

Quench not the Spirit; do not despise the
gifts of prophecy' (I Thess. 5:19–20)

INTRODUCTION

THE DRAMA of the Council of Chalcedon (451 A.D.) which rent asunder
the Church of Christ, has been ceaselessly repeated, weakening Christendom.
Through its failure to take into consideration the cultural divergences between
peoples, that Council condemned and excluded from the Body of Christ the
churches known as monophysite. This wound, still open, has affected the
Church throughout fifteen centuries. This great length of time has had to
elapse before a pope, Paul VI, and the monophysite Patriarchs, Coptic,
Armenian and Syrian, have published joint statements, attributing this
centuries-old breach to purely cultural causes, the same faith having been
expressed differently by churches of differing cultures.

Then further, lo and behold we see popes, patriarchs, bishops and theologians, Catholic and Orthodox, calmly declaring that the *Great Schism* which
finally cut in two the Church of Christ, and which has endured for over a
thousand years, was motivated by human, temporal and political considerations, not forgetting the cultural divergences between Churches professing
substantially the same faith.

Concern for uniformity thus became the cause of the destruction of
Christian unity. People came to believe that they must give a common faith a

common expression, and each Church seeks to impose its own formulation of the truths which must be believed.

It is within this setting that the project of a universal Catechism, adopted by the Extraordinary Synod of Bishops, must be considered.

1.   WHAT IS A CATECHISM?

It is important to understand what kind of catechism is at issue. A catechism in the form of a simple inventory of truths to be believed, like the one which we learned by heart in the classroom, in the form of questions and answers, would not be a worthy object of a decision of the Extraordinary Synod of Bishops.

The true catechism must serve as a manual for the process of catechesis. Now, this process is the formation of Christians, whose conduct, thought, feeling, prayer are inspired by the Gospel of Jesus Christ, in other words by his life and his teaching. A catechism of this type can leave out nothing which pertains to the formation of Christian faith, liturgy, sacraments, discipline, morality. It is of this kind of catechism that we shall speak.

2.   THE UNIVERSAL CATECHISM AND THE YOUNG CHURCHES

We shall not consider at length here the Eastern Churches in communion with Rome, who have found that they have had imposed upon them Latin law, Latin discipline, except for a few nuances, Latin ecclesiology, Latin manuals of theology and, consequently, the Latin catechesis.

We shall pay special attention, in these pages, to the young Third World Churches, founded by the Roman church amongst peoples whose cultures were entirely different from the Latin culture. Churches which have had imposed upon them not only a Latin expression of dogmas but also Latin law, Latin liturgy and, before Vatican II, the Latin language, not to speak of the Latin ecclesiastical vestments and ornaments—foreign to them—in which their hierarchy has been decked out.

Handicapped in their apostolate to their own indigenous population, the bishops of these yougn churches have sought to endow them with a religious mode of expression, a liturgy, a liturgical language and a discipline adapted to their customs and their own cultural milieu. The Second Vatican Council, through its openness to the world and to all its cultures, has provided the providential opportunity to realise the aspirations of all the churches enjoying communion with the See of Rome.

Does the Universal Catechism encourage these aspirations? In other words, does it continue the spirit of Vatican II?

3. THE UNIVERSAL CATECHISM BARS THE WAY TO THE SPIRIT OF VATICAN II

It is certain that one council cannot, in a few years, put an end to a situation which has prevailed for centuries. Vatican II laid the foundations of a reform which must be brought about gradually, over decades, if not centuries. It marks the beginning of an opening-up process, and not its completion.

It is not surprising that such a council should come up against difficulties, or that certain people should wish to stifle in its cradle a process of reform which has hardly begun. To achieve this goal, the project we are considering is a masterly device.

In effect, to publish at the present time a Universal Catechism, a form of common and solemn profession of faith, which would benefit from the quasi-infallible approval of the pope, would mean freezing the decrees of the Council, which are now only in a projected form, into a quasi-definitive formulation, which would make them the final term of a reform which has so far hardly been sketched out. It would cut short the researches undertaken by those bishops who are directly involved, by the theologians, the liturgists and the jurists concerned to set the Council on the path of concrete realisations, and would establish the existing *de facto* situation and bind the Church for many years to come to the present thinking, which is still so similar to the past, of the Council.

4. CAN THE ROMAN CHURCH FORMULATE A UNIVERSAL CATECHISM?

For a catechism to be able to be called universal, it must emanate from the universal Church, that is from the whole Church, it must be intended for all Christians and it must draw its inspiration from the universal Christian tradition. Now, the Roman church, which is limited in fact, and in essence, to the Latin church, is one particular church, which intends for the use of Catholics alone a catechism which is inspired by one particular tradition, the Latin one. This catechism cannot then be called universal.

The Orthodox tradition, both theological, liturgical, juridical and ascetic, constitutes an integral—and not the least important—part of the Christian tradition. Any religious activity or institution which ignores it cannot be universal, any more than a council held by the Roman church, in the absence of Eastern Orthodoxy, can be universal or ecumenical. Is this not what Pope Paul VI wished to imply when, in his message, issued on the occasion of the celebration of the seven hundredth anniversary of the Council of Lyons, he described that council as the sixth of the General Synods of the West?

5.   IS IT APPROPRIATE THAT THE ROMAN CHURCH SHOULD FORMULATE A CATHOLIC CATECHISM TO BE IMPOSED UPON THE EASTERN UNIATE CHURCHES?

No! For if the Eastern Catholics share the faith of the Roman church, they are not always obliged to share the Latin formulation of that faith, a formulation which must be revised by the reunited Catholic and Orthodox Churches, in the light of the universal tradition. Furthermore, a true catechesis must be centred upon the Eucharist; the Eastern Uniate Churches, possessing their own eucharistic and sacramental liturgy, cannot purely and simply adopt a catechism of Latin inspiration.

6.   IS IT APPROPRIATE THAT THE ROMAN CHURCH SHOULD FORMULATE A 'UNIVERSAL CATECHISM' TO BE IMPOSED UPON THE WHOLE LATIN CHURCH?

This is equally impossible! Both on the ecumenical and on the pastoral level.

a. On the ecumenical level: Vatican II has opened an era of dialogue with Eastern Orthodoxy and a mixed commission has been set up to seek to reduce the divergences which exist between the Roman and Orthodox churches, and to enable these churches to agree on a common formulation of truths which are the subject of dispute. A catechism of this importance, created unilaterally by the Roman church and enshrining the Latin formulation, would impede the work of this commission and give the impression that the Church of Rome does not take seriously this dialogue with Orthodoxy.

b. On the pastoral level: It is unthinkable that the Catholic church, after Vatican II, should wish to impose a uniform catechism, Latin in inspiration, on the young churches of the Third World, founded by the Roman church and whose culture is totally different from the Latin culture.

In effect, Christianity is not a pure ideology. It is *a person to person relationship*, of the soul to Christ. It is a communion of life, which supposes a direct exchange, in which Christ and man give and receive. If the Son of God has given himself to the soul, he insists on reciprocity: 'My son, give me your heart!' (Prov. 23:26).

Now, this reciprocal love is a participation in the life of the Trinity. Christ loves us with the same love with which the Father loves him: 'As the Father has loved me, so also I have loved you' (John 15:9). And, addressing the Father, Jesus cries: 'O Father, I have made your Name known to them, and I will make it known again, so that the love with which you have loved me may be in them, and I in them' (John 17:26). Christ descends among us, in the place where we live: 'I will come in to him'. He spreads his table within our heart: 'I shall come in to him and sup with him, and he with me' (Rev. 3:20).

In short, Christ takes our nature upon himself as we are, where we are, with our temperament, our hereditary habits, our physical and intellectual constitution, and cultural and social inheritance. With the result that each human being must have his Christ, made in his image and likeness, and whom he knows and loves through his own soul. Each soul has its own story of Jesus, its own Gospel which it reads and assimilates in its own way.

The evangelists, who knew the same Jesus Christ, directly or through intermediaries, have recounted his life in different ways. It is the same Christ, but projected onto the soul of each one of them. Each has retained of Christ's life and words what most impressed him, what his soul has most thoroughly assimilated, and has related, in his gospel, that part of it which was most appropriate for his readers. Thus it is that we have four gospels, four lives of Jesus Christ, which complete and enrich each other reciprocally.

There are, then, as many ways of encountering the Gospel, of reading it and living it, in other words, *as many ways of being a Christian, as there are ways of living, thinking, speaking, feeling and reacting.* The catechetical process must, therefore, to instruct a people, make use of their own language, their traditions, their culture, their soul. It must adapt Christ to fit that people's natural form. Saint Paul reminded the Galatians that, through baptism, they had put on Christ as a garment: 'All of you who have been baptised in Christ, have put on Christ' (Gal. 3:27). Now, to clothe the baptised person in Christ, it is necessary to adapt Christ to his natural form. And if the Apostle Paul became all things to all men and adapted himself to each human community which he evangelised, in order to save it (I Cor. 9:19–23), how much more must his Master become all things to all men in order to save them all? Can he fail to make himself black among the black races, in order to win the blacks, and yellow among the yellow races, to win the yellow, and so on, he who 'emptied himself, taking the form of a slave, being made in the likeness of men' (Phil. 2:7)?

Like Christ, its head, the Church is not universal because it numbers among its followers black, yellow and white people, but because it offers all these peoples a Christ of their own race, able to identify with them in order to identify them with himself. A Christ who was incapable of being one of their own would not be their Christ, their Saviour, their incarnate Word, 'flesh of their flesh, bone of their bone'. Have we not seen every people paint or sculpt in its own image and its own colour its own Christ and its own Virgin?

One may force on the young Churches a uniform Latin catechism, but they will then have a borrowed faith; one may force on their believers a Roman or Western Christ and one may install him on their altars, but he will remain a stranger to their souls, and their inner adherence will be liable to all manner of instability.

Each church must therefore be helped to make its own Christ, soul of its soul and life of its life; it must be helped to construct its own liturgy, its own prayers, its own Gospel of Jesus Christ; *we must help each church to compose its own catechism for itself*, that is, to live its own Christian life, within the boundaries of the common faith.

Vatican II intended to open itself up to all peoples, to adapt the Church to all cultures and all civilisations. It has hardly begun to realise its ambitions. Must it be confronted with a uniform catechism, labelled universal, which would bind the Church, for a long time to come, to a present state of affairs which is so similar to the past, and would block all those efforts which are being made to secure the reforms and readaptations envisaged by the Council?

Christianity was born in a Graeco-Roman world which already possessed its own advanced civilisation, and which marked it with its own philosophy and culture, just as it marked the Church, from Constantine onwards, with its imperialist spirit; so much so that Pope John XXIII spoke of 'shaking off the dust which has accumulated, since the time of Constantine, on the throne of Saint Peter'. Thanks to the Roman church, we are witnessing today the birth and the growth of Christianity in a Third World which has little to give and much to receive. Let us allow it to work freely in these lands which have only just been brought under cultivation and to mark these still virgin peoples with a truly evangelical culture, which does not contain the seeds of a civilisation which is too materialistic and rationalist and is today gnawing away at the Christian West.

These young Churches might one day have the task of re-evangelising the West which is in the midst of a crisis of faith and morality.

Translated by Lawrence H. Ginn

Berard Marthaler

The Synod and the Catechism

1. THE SYNOD AND THE CATECHISM

IT HAS been said that the most significant action taken by the Extraordinary Synod of Bishops commemorating the twentieth anniversary of the Second Vatican Council was its recommendation that 'a catechism or compendium of all Catholic doctrine regarding both faith and morals be composed, that it might be, as it were, a point of reference for the catechisms or compendiums that are prepared in the various regions' (p. 52). If it sees the light of day and *if it is well done*, such a compendium—as its advocates expect—will shape the mind of the Church for decades, perhaps centuries, to come.

The idea for a universal catechism did not arise spontaneously in the aula of the Synod; for several years it had been a topic of discussion and even the centre of some controversy. The Synod's recommendation raises, moreover, a question about the *relationship of the Extraordinary Synod to the Second Vatican Council, which rejected proposals for a universal catechism in favour of a General Catechetical Directory*! In calling for a universal catechism did the Extraordinary Synod implicitly repudiate a position taken by Vatican II? Or is its recommendation different from the proposals rejected by the Council? In order to answer these questions it is necessary first to review previous proposals for a universal catechism.

2. DE PARVO CATECHISMO

The idea of a uniform catechism for the universal church was conceived at the time of Vatican I.[1]

A draft of the *Constitution on a Small Catechism* was approved successively by the Commission on Church Discipline (September 30, 1869) and the Central Commission (October 18). The opening paragraph read as follows:

> Just as all members of the Church of Christ, spread over the whole world, should be of one heart and soul, so too should they have but one voice and tongue. And since different methods and ways of transmitting to the faithful the essentials of faith are known to create no little inconvenience, we shall by our own authority and with the approval of this council, see to it that a new catechism is drawn up in Latin, modelled after the *Small Catechism* of the Ven. Cardinal Bellarmine. Compiled at the command of this Holy See, it is highly recommended to all the local ordinaries. Its use by all will facilitate the disappearance in the future of the confusing variety of other short catechisms.

The schema went on to direct that it be translated into vernacular languages, that priests explain it, and that copies be put in the hands of all the faithful 'who can easily commit it to memory'. Then it continued,

> Although the use of the aforementioned short catechism is to be faithfully upheld, bishops will still be free to issue in separate form whatever catechetical instructions they deem appropriate...

It closed urging 'as strongly as we can' that all clergy charged with the care of souls make use of the Catechism of the Council of Trent. 'In this way', it said, 'there will be one common rule for transmitting the faith and for training the Christian people in all the works of piety.'

The proposal elicited an unexpectedly spirited debate on the floor of the council. Most favoured the idea, but for varying reasons. Some opposed it, primarily on the basis of their own pastoral experience and the traditional right of the diocesan bishop to develop his own catechism. After six full days of debate the proposal was sent back to the Commission on Discipline which prepared a second draft. In presenting the revised draft for a vote a commission spokesman made it clear that the schema was concerned only with a catechism to be used in elementary instruction. With that clarification *De parvo catechismo* was approved with 491 voting *placet*, 44 *plaet juxta modum*, and 56 *non placet*. After some minor revisions were made in light of the *modi*, the new text was read in the aula, but a vote was never taken due to the indefinite postponement of the Council in October following the outbreak of war between France and Germany the previous July.

3. THE GENERAL CATECHETICAL DIRECTORY

When bishops and others were asked to send in proposals which might be considered at the Second Vatican Council, Bishop Pierre-Marie Lacointe of

Beauvais correctly predicted that some would urge a return to the unfinished work of Vatican I. Bishop Lacointe argued, however, that a single catechism for the whole Church was not possible or, at least, not proper. He recommended instead directives for the catechesis of different classes of children and adults. In the period 1961–62 two commissions—the preparatory Commission for the Eastern Churches and the preparatory Commission on Discipline—drafted schemata which called for a new catechism.[2]

In the course of time the Commission on Discipline came to the conclusion that *a single catechism for the universal Church was not feasible* because conditions differ so greatly from country to country and individual to individual. On the other hand, it *also opposed the proliferation of catechisms* which would result from each diocese having its own. Following the suggestion of Bishop Lacointe, the commission adopted the idea of a *catechetical directory* that would establish general 'rules and norms, which would have to be observed in compiling individual catechisms'. It would address the goals catechesis, the principal tenets of doctrine, and the wording of formulas. Such a directory would leave the application of the general norms in specific situations to the episcopal conferences. In the end their recommendation was be observed in compiling individual catechisms'. It would address the goals of Bishops'. Article 44 of the decree, something of a catchall, presented a general mandate prescribing, among other things, a general catechetical directory.

In opting for a *general catechetical directory instead of a universal catechism*, Vatican II signalled an *advance beyond the understanding of catechesis prevalent in the nineteenth century*. The catechism proposed at Vatican I was for children—elementary instruction—whereas the proposals of Vatican II moved away from book-centered catechesis to catechesis as a whole. Besides the directory Vatican II called for professional training for catechists, a restoration of the catechumenate and the recognition of the close relationship between catechesis and the celebration of the liturgy. A 'small catechism' no matter how well designed simply could not be the principal instrument of catechetical renewal.

4. THE SYNODS OF 1967 AND 1977

The general directory was still to be published when the first post-conciliar Synod of Bishops met in 1967, and the *issue of a catechism came up again* during the discussion on 'dangerous opinions and atheism'. Many bishops thought the best way to counteract error and confusion would be by means of a public statement. Some wanted the synod or the pope to issue a magisterial document in the tradition of the great encyclicals of John XXIII and Paul VI;

it should not be simply a dry list of truths to be believed or errors to be avoided. Some supported the publication of a 'rule of faith' that would enumerate in a positive way and adapt to the modern mentality the fundamental truths of faith. Some proposed an explanatory work to be written by specialists. Others preferred, however, a catechism—perhaps an updated version of that of Trent, or better, a catechism of Vatican II, written and published by the *magisterium* with the help of experts. A couple of voices spoke against the publication of catechisms and documents, maintaining that the time was not ripe to settle certain questions or opinions thought to be dangerous.[3]

It is clear from the interventions, however, that the bishops who spoke in favour of a new or revised catechism had in mind a work quite different from the small catechism discussed at Vatican I.[4] *The issue was no longer the elementary instruction of children but the misconceptions and confusion of grown-ups.* The 1967 synod said nothing about a catechism in its final report because, it was thought, the matter had already been taken care of in some manner by the mandate in *Christus Dominus* that called for a catechetical directory.[5] Before the synod adjourned, however, Cardinal Villot, then prefect of the Congregation for the Clergy, gave a progress report regarding the directory. The General Catechetical Directory was finally published almost four years later in June, 1971.

The theme of the synod of 1977 was 'catechesis in our time'. Although it put special emphasis on catechesis for children and young people, the synod had *very little to say about catechisms of any kind, let alone a universal catechism.* The *instrumentum laboris*—the 'working paper'—based on responses to the questionaire sent to the national hierarchies, referred to catechetical methods of the past and in particular to the role played by the catechism and the memorizing of it (par. 13). This paragraph was the focus of the intervention of Archbishop Dermot Ryan of Dublin speaking in the name of the Irish Episcopal Conference. He argued the case for children to memorise certain formulas—creeds, standard prayers, the parts of the Mass, the Decalogue, Beatitudes, gifts of the Holy Spirit and precepts of the Church. Archbishop Ryan, however, prefaced his remarks saying: 'It would be too much to expect the synod to produce a catechism which would be short, containing the essentials, and revised in the light of Vatican Council II and subsequent documents of the *magisterium*. Perhaps the time is not ripe for beginning such a work.'[6]

Although one suspects that Archbishop Ryan favoured a catechism, there was little support for it among other bishops at the 1977 synod. Several spoke to the importance of systematic catechesis and the need to memorise formulas, but their main concern went well beyond the instruments and organisation of catechesis to the nature and scope of the task and its relationship to evangelisation. The bishops summarised their principal concerns in thirty-four propositions which were forwarded to the pope, but *none of the propositions contained a recommendation regarding the publication of a catechism*. In his closing address Paul VI endorsed 'the necessity of some fundamental formulas which will make it possible to express more easily, in a suitable and accurate way, the truths of the faith and of Christian moral doctrine', but he too was silent regarding a catechism.

Pope Paul died in August, 1978 and it was left to Pope John Paul II, who as cardinal-archbishop of Krakow had been a participant in the proceedings, to issue the Apostolic Exhortation *Catechesi tradendae* based on the work of the synod. *Catechesi tradendae* reaffirmed the importance of the General Cate-chetical Directory saying that it 'is still the basic document for encouraging and guiding catechetical renewal throughout the Church' (par. 2). It should be noted that the General Directory gives *guidelines for the preparation and publication of catechisms* (par. 119, 134) because Pope John Paul again cites the directory when stating:

> I must warmly encourage the episcopal conferences of the whole world to under-take, patiently but resolutely, the considerable work to be accomplished in agree-ment with the Apostolic See in order to prepare genuine catechisms which will be faithful to the essential content of educating the Christian generations of the future to a sturdy faith. (par. 50)

While obviously promoting the use of catechisms, the text *says nothing about a single catechism for the universal Church*, but rather seems to allow for some adaptation to local needs.

5. THE EXTRAORDINARY SYNOD OF 1985

That the Extraordinary Synod called by Pope John Paul II to commemor-ate the twentieth anniversary of the Second Vatican Council would once more take up the issue of the catechism was hinted at even before the bishops convened. In his summary of the responses to the questionnaire sent out by the General Secretariat of the Synod Cardinal Danneels, relator of the Synod, noted that in some countries there is evidence of a kind of *selective Christiani-ty*—a certain lack of integrity and organic structure in catechesis. Some episcopal conferences, therefore, spoke of a catechism which would meet the needs of the post Vatican II Church in the way that the Roman Catechism addressed the needs of the Church after the Council of Trent.[7]

About half the interventions, as published in summary form in *L'Osserva-*

tore Romano, said something about *catechesis*—often noting progress and advances in cultural adaptation—but only a few mentioned *a catechism*. Cardinal Law, archbishop of Boston, was the first publicly to advocate a universal catechism:

> I propose a Commission of Cardinals to prepare a draft of a Conciliar Catechism to be promulgated by the Holy Father after consulting the bishops of the world. In a shrinking world—a global village—*national* catechisms will not fill the current need for clear articulation of the Church's faith.

The following day Bishop Ruhuna of Burundi requested 'a model catechism, inspired by Vatican II'. On the other hand, the intervention of the Latin Patriarch of Jerusalem, Giacomo Beltritti, seemed to echo the debate of Vatican I when he advocated a single catechism for children to be used in the entire Church, adaptable to the needs of various countries.

After the ninth general congregation of the Synod (November 29) *the discussions shifted to small study groups*, divided according to languages, where the *proposal for a 'catechism' began to crystallise*. The Italian language group recommended the publication of three works to promote the knowledge of Vatican II: a 'Catechism of the Faith' directed towards believers; a 'Book of Christian Faith', for non-believers; and a 'Book of Moral Doctrine' for everyone. The English language study group A urged 'a compendium of Catholic teaching from which each country could draw its own teaching documents'. Similarly the French study group B recommended 'a catechism or compendium' containing the teachings of Vatican II. It added that the catechism should take care to present Jesus Christ as the object and centre of catechesis and that the Gospel should be presented as a way of life and not as an ideology.

The Spanish language study group B wanted the Holy See, after consulting with the conferences of bishops, to undertake the preparation of a reference work of Catholic teaching, a compendium of synthetic formulations of faith and morals. They made it clear that they were asking not for a detailed catechism but for a complete synthesis of Church teaching regarding faith and morals presented with the new pastoral insights of Vatican II. The Latin study group endorsed the idea of a universal catechism according to Vatican II like the one that was done after the Council of Trent. In compiling such a catechism they wanted Pope Paul VI's profession of faith to be taken into consideration because it must be regarded as the principal directive in producing new catechism texts.

The reports of the study groups are especially important for understanding the basis and intent of the recommendation which appeared in the final report of the Extraordinary Synod:

Very many have expressed the desire that a catechism or compendium of all Catholic doctrine regarding both faith and morals be composed, that it might be, as it were, a point of reference for the catechisms or compendiums that are prepared in the various regions. The presentation of doctrine must be biblical and liturgical. It must be sound doctrine suited to the present life of Christians (II, B.4).

In the context of both the interventions of individual bishops and the discussions in the language groups, it is evident that the *'catechism or compendium' requested by the Extraordinary Synod is quite different from the small catechism proposed at Vatican I and rejected by Vatican II in favour of the General Catechetical Directory.* The recommendation of the Synod differs from the schema *De parvo catechismo* of Vatican I in two important respects: first, it seems to envisage a work for *mature readers*, primarily catechists, teachers and other pastoral leaders, charged with the instruction of the faithful; and second, the Synod acknowledges *cultural diversity* and the need to adapt to regional differences.

The desire for a catechism which would interpret and diffuse the teachings of the Second Vatican Council such as the *Catechismus ad parochos* propagated the teachings of the Council of Trent was expressed by some at the 1967 synod, but it took almost twenty years for the idea to germinate. The Latin language group at the Extraordinary Synod claimed that such a catechism had already been proposed while Vatican II was still in session, but, if indeed that were the case, the proposal never received formal consideration. Certainly, the *recommendation of the 1985 Synod does not run contrary to any action taken at Vatican II.* In so far as it makes allowance for cultural differences and implies that the catechesis of adults is the chief form of all catechesis (GCD, par. 20), the 'catechism or compendium of Catholic doctrine' is in the best tradition of the General Directory which, as Pope John Paul II has said, 'is still the basic document for encouraging and guiding catechetical renewal throughout the Church'.

Notes

1. I follow the account of Michael T. Donnellan *Rationale for a Uniform Catechism: Vatican I to Vatican II.* Unpublished doctoral dissertation at the Catholic University of America, Washington, D.C., 1972.

2. The documentation for this section can be found in B.L. Marthaler *Catechetics in Context.* Notes and Commentary on the General Catechetical Director (Huntington, IN. 1972) pp. xvi–xxx.

3. G. Caprile *Il sinodo dei vescovi* (Rome 1968) p. 221.

4. Caprile, the work cited in note 3, at pp. 190, 197, 209.

5. Caprile, the work cited in note, 3 at pp. 226, 562.

6. The full text of Archbishop Ryan's intervention appears in *The Living Light* 15 (1978) 45–47.

7. At the time of writing the most complete collection of synodal documents is the French *Synode Extraordinaire. Celebration de Vatican II* (Paris 1986). It must, however, be supplemented with other sources when available; for example, the reference to the catechism, found in the Latin original, it curiously omitted in the French version (see p. 345).

Hermann Pottmeyer

The Church as Mysterium and as Institution

1. THE MEDIA REACTION TO THE SYNOD

THE GERMAN weekly *Die Zeit* headed its assessment of the Special Synod 'Flight into the mysterium'. Its view was that the concept of 'mysterium' was put forth in the Synod assembly as a theological code-word, enabling the participants to breath more freely; it allowed the bishops to avoid the real problems, not least a debate on essential structural reforms, which a number of bishops' conferences had called for.[1]

Many commentators observed that it was above all the 'conservative' German cardinals, Ratzinger, Höffner (Cologne) and Meisner (Berlin), who had introduced the term 'mysterium'. In doing so they had voiced their criticism of the postconciliar debates on structure, which they felt to be excessive. A counterpoise was provided by the representatives of the English-speaking churches in particular, led by Cardinal Hume; under the motif of 'communio' they called for structural reforms, especially the broadening of collegiality. The Church in the 'Third World', it was felt, identified a certain common cause with them here; the latter were looking for a more independent development of local churches under the heading of 'enculturation'.

It is a fact that *'mysterium' and 'communio' are the ecclesiological motifs of the Special Synod*. The first refers to the real *theological aspect*, the second to the *institutional aspect* of the Church. But does 'mysterium' indicate a new trend in the postconciliar development? We can only attempt an answer if we compare the *Sitz-im-leben* of 'mysterium' in the Special Synod with that in the Council. For, like 'communio', 'mysterium' is also a fundamental ecclesiological motif of the Council.

2. THE CONTEXT OF 'MYSTERIUM' IN THE SYNOD

The *Sitz-im-leben* of 'mysterium' language in the Special Synod can first of all be ascertained from the bishops' own contributions. The proposal to stress the 'mysterium' aspect of the Church, which came particularly from the German bishops, *initially reflects the postconciliar situation of the Church in Germany*. The German talent for organisation and thoroughness, economic prosperity, a high income from the Church Tax and an extended discussion (and reform) of structures, have led to a whole sequence of levels of consultation, a high degree of organisation and an inflation of the Church's bureaucratic apparatus. Bishops and priests are overburdened by organisational and bureaucratic tasks. Since, at the same time, there is a decrease in the number of priests and active Church members, many have come to see the Church 'as a depersonalised organisation. The ecclesiastical apparatus obscures the Church as *mysterium*. That is why so many young people leave the Church and go to the sects which flourish among the young'. This is Cardinal Meisner's analysis.[2] He suggests that 'we need once again to let people see the Church as the Mystical Body of Christ, the Bride of Christ and Mother of Believers, i.e., in its mystical dimension within mankind. This will give it a personal, human face, which will invite and attract people .... It is our inheritance that Christ can be seen in the face of the Church; but it is also our continuing task.'

Cardinal Höffner criticised 'the many who put their hope in altering structures and conditions, whereas the Church's real renewal consists in the changing of hearts and in people turning to God'.[3] He pointed, in contrast, to the Council's teaching of the Church as the sacrament of salvation. Cardinal Ratzinger's long-standing critique of the way the Church in Germany has become 'synodalised' and bureaucratised is well known. At the Special Synod he complained that, for many people today, 'the Church has been reduced to its institutional aspect. It is essential, therefore, to put forward the Church as *mysterium*, transcending itself towards Christ. The Synod cannot make the distribution of power its primary topic'.[4]

There is a *second prong* to the German bishops' emphasis on the Church as *mysterium*. By contrast with the so-called optimism in *Gaudium et Spes*, which Cardinal Ratzinger had already criticised as 'naïve' many years ago[5], there is a decidedly *critical evaluation of the contemporary situation*. Thus Cardinal Höffner: 'The present crisis in the Church is widely due to the secularised world being imported into it, above all in the form of spiralling emancipation, subjectivism, horizontalism and consumerism'. Both views, the reduction of the Church to its institutional and structural aspect, and the danger of secularism, were also taken up in the report of the German-speaking working-party.[6]

Thus behind the German bishops' proposal to emphasise the Church as *mysterium* there is initially a postconciliar experience and a pastoral concern. Whether tactical considerations also played a part here, as the media assumed, echoing the danger of a 'restoration' movement which had been mooted in advance of the Synod, is something that cannot be ascertained or suggested here. What is unmistakable is the fact that for the present the German bishops attach no pastoral importance to a further broadening of Church structures. Here they differ from participants from the English-speaking world and the 'Third World'. Cardinal Hume, leading on from the clear-cut statement of the Bishops' Conference of England and Wales, stressed the importance of the concept of 'communio' as an ecclesiological category, its pastoral significance in a changing society and its structural consequences; communio-structures should be further developed at all levels of Church life.[7] This view was also put forward by Bishop Malone as a representative of the Bishops' Conference of the U.S.A.[8]

Unmistakably, the *Central European bishops' analysis of the situation was adopted* in the final report of the Special Synod. This is doubtless due to the close collaboration of the Belgian Cardinal Danneels, who drew up the report, and the Synod's secretary, the German Professor Walter Kasper. The fact that a final report could be published at all is due to them. The main themes of the analysis of contemporary conditions in section I4 and IIA are secularism and a one-sidedly sociological view of the Church which emphasises its institutional aspect.[9] The Synod sees a sign of hope in a growing 'return to the holy' which is making itself felt in a new hunger and thirst for transcendence, in the eruption of spiritual movements in the Church, but also in the spread of the sects. So the Synod sees itself challenged to present the Church primarily as *mysterium*.

What is said about the Church as *mysterium* in section IIA corresponds to chapters I, V, VII and VIII of *Lumen Gentium*, which it expressly quotes. The christocentric and trinitarian character of Vatican II's ecclesiology is underlined. A deepened spirituality and the witness of holiness are enjoined upon pastors and laity. The view is that the Church can only become more worthy of belief if it bears witness that Christ Crucified is its life. Anyone criticising the concluding Synod report for taking the Church as *mysterium* as its starting-point has failed to see that *Lumen Gentium* also begins with this same aspect. Furthermore, as has been shown many times in recent years, it is precisely those chapters of *Lumen Gentium* which the Synod report underlined that have received too little attention so far. It is high time for a spiritual deepening of the postconciliar renewal.[10]

However, the context in which this view of the Church as *mysterium* is situated, namely the Synod's two-pronged approach, does give rise to *critical questions*. Is it sufficient to analyse the modern world in terms of 'secularism' (an autonomistic view of man and the world, immanentism, consumerism)? Does the brief acknowledgment of a legitimate autonomy of temporal things in *Gaudium et Spes* constitute an adequate counterpoise? Is it really correct to dismiss as naïve and optimistic everything to which the Pastoral Constitution paid tribute in terms of the advance of human freedom? For this is an ongoing process, endangered both from within and from without, and needs positive support on the part of Christians. Has the Church taken the increased awareness of freedom (and the resultant change in man's whole approach) seriously enough in its pastoral practice and in the shape of its structures? Is it right to generalise our European experience of the increased estrangement of the Church from people and to seek the fault only on one side? It would be unjust to ignore the change that has taken place in and through the Church since Vatican II. In many nations and in numerous areas of life, today's Church is a sign of hope for people who are striving to live in freedom in a way that is more worthy of the human being. This great gain must not be endangered by the tendency to dismiss the world as the domain of the 'prince of this world'14. It is the mystery of the triune God's economy of salvation, in particular, that asserts that God's Spirit is also at work outside the Church, not least in the just striving for freedom and the development of indigenous cultural values.

This brings us to the second prong. It is right to link the postconciliar discussion of structures and the desire for a further structural broadening with a one-sidedly sociological view which sees the Church as a mere emanation of autonomistic emancipation? Surely this is biased? It is true that the revitalising of synodal forms has resulted in misunderstandings, in particular their confusion with the political model of democracy. It is also true that the Synod committees are flogging a dead horse and becoming, in their turn, mere bureaucratic machines if they come up with utterances which are isolated from the life of the community and the Church. This may be particularly true in Germany, with its perfect ecclesiastical organisation, on the one hand, and its falling active church membership, on the other. All the same we must not lose sight of the fact that, for instance, the suggestions of the Bishops' Conference of England and Wales on the broadening of collegiality and participation under the motif of 'communio', and the desire for greater attention to the principle of subsidiarity and for more delegation of power to national churches, spring from eminently pastoral concerns. It is all the more significant, then, that Pope John Paul II, in his address at the concluding session of the Synod, laid striking emphasis on the bishops' responsibility for the whole Church and, quoting Paul VI, affirmed that they should have a greater role in governing the whole Church as an expression of collegiality. At the same time he recommended the holding of synods, with wide participation of the faithful in their preparation.[11]

Finally it must be seen that the Church's credibility is promoted not only by the holy lives of its members but, no less, by manifesting itself as a true *communio ecclesiarum* and *communio fidelium*, as a unity in diversity. Elsewhere the final Synod report puts this well: 'The Church as *communio* is a sacrament for the salvation of the world' (IID1).

3. THE CONTEXT OF 'MYSTERIUM' IN THE COUNCIL

In discussing the Church as *mysterium*, did the Synod adopt the *letter* only, or *also the spirit of the Council*? What was the context of this idea during the Council and in the Council documents?

The history of the teaching which describes the Church as mysterium-sacrament, and in particular its context in Vatican II, has been most exhaustively explored by L. Boff.[12] *Vatican II follows two lines of thought.* On the one hand its view of the Church is directed against the triumphalism, clericalism and juridicism of the Counter-Reformation and Neo-Scholastic ecclesiology, as Bishop de Smedt stated in the aula on 1.12.1962.[13] The Church sees itself as relative both to Jesus Christ who is the primordial sacrament of salvation, and to the salvation and unity of mankind, which the Church is sent to serve.[14] The Council's second line of thought is to determine the locus and task of the Church in this particular phase of history when the world is increasingly seen as a 'planet'. The Church's sphere of life is no longer a homogeneous Christendom but a humanity which 'is tending more and more towards civil, economic and social unity' (LG 281 cf. LG 1). Thus the Council understands the Church as a 'sacrament—a sign and instrument, that is, of communion with God and of unity among all men' (LG 1). As the sacrament for the unity of mankind its ministry 'amounts to an effective living of faith and love, not to any external power exercised by purely human means' (GS 42).

At an early stage Y. Congar and K. Rahner pointed out the systematic significance of the doctrine of the Church as mysterium-sacrament.[15] The Council adopts the whole spectrum of meanings which the concept mysterium-sacrament has unfolded down through the history of theology. In the Church Fathers, and based on the New Testament, 'mysterium' originally referred to the unfathomable economy of salvation, into which the Church, a creation of the triune God, is drawn. 'Mysterium' is also used to describe the person of Jesus Christ, the events of his life, his foreshadowing in the Old Covenant and finally the Eucharist and baptism. In accord with this, the Fathers also speak of the Church itself as *mysterium* and sacrament since it is a sign and instrument of the divine saving revelation. Only later, in the Latin Church, was the concept of 'sacrament' restricted to the seven sacraments.[16]

The ancient Church's doctrine of mysterium-sacrament is designed to bring out *a general structure of the economy of salvation*: the invisible God shows himself in and works through the visible. It is in this sense that the Council, too, speaks of the Church as 'sacrament'. The term designates 'the way in which the visible and the invisible, the divine and the human are linked; for in the christological order of salvation each postulates and upholds the other reciprocally: there is a real distinction between the two elements, the visible element is necessary (*medii*) in view of the pneumatic dimension, and the pneumatic can exist in many different elements'.[17] Thus the official commentary reads: 'Vox "mysterium" non simpliciter indicat aliquid incognoscibile aut abstrusum, sed . . . designat realitatem divinam transcendentem et salvificam, quae aliquo modo visibili revelatur et manifestatur'.[18] In the famous words of the Council the Church forms 'one complex reality which comes together from a human and a divine element' (LG 8).

The designation of the Church as sacrament is of great structural relevance. For it demands that the *visible form and organisation of the Church correspond to its ground and life-principle*, i.e., the mystery of the triune God, the mystery of Jesus Christ and the mystery of the Spirit's working. The Council was well aware of this implication when it replaced the clerical and centralist model of the Church by the structural motif of 'communio': as *communio*, the Church is the fruit of the triune God's communio with men; it images the *communio* of Father, Son and Holy Spirit (cf. LG 4; UR 7). The Council goes on to apply the theologico-structural concept 'communio' to all areas of the Church's life: it is a *communio fidelium* in the People of God, *communio hierarchica* in the college of bishops, *communio ecclesiarum* in the whole Church; it is unity in diversity, and *communio non plena* with the separated churches. For the Council, therefore, there is the closest possible relationship between the Church as mysterium-sacrament and the Church as *communio*.

As regards the Synod it is not without interest that the doctrine of the Church as mysterium-sacrament—which had almost been forgotten since the time of the Church Fathers—was developed by nineteenth and twentieth century German theology.[19] The teaching was taken up in the 30's of the present century by Y. Congar and H. de Lubac.[20] Its adoption at the Council was due in large measure to the efforts of German bishops, led by Cardinals Döpfner (Berlin) and Frings (Cologne), with the assistance of the theologians

K. Rahner and J. Ratzinger.[21] It was the draft provided by German bishops and theologians which 'had the greatest influence—as regards the Church as sacrament—on the final texts of the dogmatic constitution on the Church'.[22]

4. A COMPARISON OF THE TWO CONTEXTS

This fact invites comparison of the respective contexts of this teaching of the Church as mysterium-sacrament in the Synod and in the Council. In adverting to this doctrine, the German participants of the Synod were drawing upon the best ecclesiological tradition of their country, which had already proved fruitful in the structural reform of the Church by the Council. Citing this doctrine in order to emphasise the Church's spiritual reality, they were entirely in accord with the teaching of the Council. Yet there is an *unmistakable shift in direction*, in two respects. First with regard to the 'signs of the times': whereas the Council saw the world's 'planetary' growing-together pointing to the same destination as the Church, with its task of being the sacrament of mankind's unity—hence 'elevating the sociological point of departure to the level of a theological one'[23]—the German participants at the Synod and, influenced by them, the concluding Synod report, see the world's process of unification as being profoundly disturbed: 'Fear and oppression have increased. Throughout the whole world there is a growth of famine, repression, injustice and war, torture, terrorism and other forms of violence' (IID1). The Council's view, which suggested that the history of mankind and salvation-history ran parallel, is now seen to be problematical; it is matched by the counterpoint of a *theology of the cross*. 'It seems to us that, through today's difficulties, God is leading us to a deeper awareness of the value, meaning and centrality of the cross of Jesus Christ. Thus the relation of mankind's history to salvation-history needs to be explained in the light of the Easter mystery' (IID2). This, however, the document goes on, is not a pessimistic view of things, but the realism of Christian hope. This is accordingly emphasised in the section on the mystery of the Church: 'Thus the mystery of the cross and that of the resurrection are always simultaneously present in the Church' (IIA3).

There are unmistakable *echoes here of the debate on 'liberation theology'* and its view of the relation between mankind's history and salvation-history (cf. IID6). We need to remember that sacramental ecclesiology played a significant part in the working-out of 'liberation theology'. So L. Boff, as a result of his examination of German and conciliar theology of the Church as sacrament, arrived at his manifesto: 'the "Church" as total sacrament is a concept which belongs to the theology of revolution'.[24] Just as it warns against the identification of the history of mankind and the history of salvation, the concluding Synod report warns against a false concept of 'aggiornamento' in certain postconciliar tendencies: 'It is this Easter perspective, which confirms the unity of cross and resurrection, that can help us distinguish the true meaning of the so-called *aggiornamento* from the false. It excludes a trivialising and uncritical assimilation, which could lead to a secularising of the Church' (IID3).

No doubt the Synod was right to take note of the shift which has taken place since the Council with regard to the 'signs of the times' and which, under the heading of 'post-modern' developments, has been the subject of some reflection. However, 'secularism' is an inadequate term to describe how many people have become estranged from the Church. The Church's social environment is much more heterogeneous and calls for a new model of the relation between Church and society. While it is right to say that what is needed is the testimony of a holy life, the next question is, 'How does a holy life manifest itself today?' In speaking of the Church as *mysterium* we must not remain abstract, attempting to lift the Church out of the sphere of historical developments. The mystery of the Church, the mystery of the cross and resurrection of Jesus Christ, actually indicates the Church's place within history. One of the reasons for the alienation of many people from the Church, and for many conflicts within the Church itself, is that we have not yet discovered an appropriate model for the relation between the Church and a society which is attempting to develop according to the ideal of responsible self-determination—or at least, such a model has as yet no clear outline and in any case has to take different forms in the particular Churches. The efforts being made in this direction must not be stigmatised at the outset as sociologism or 'secularising the Church'. The fact that the particular Churches see themselves called to try new paths in their own environments is precisely the pastoral concern which has been enunciated in terms of 'communio' in many of the statements of bishops' conferences and in many of the contributions made at the Synod.

There has been a further change since the Council. It concerns the weight attributed to the *structural implications of the doctrine of the Church as mysterium-sacrament*. Whereas the Council's communio-ecclesiology yielded a synodal movement and structural creativity, the Synod's statements are guarded in this area. The concluding report is even prepared to see the reason for young people's antipathy to the institutional Church in the fact that 'we have spoken too much about renewing the external structures of the Church and too little about God and Christ'*. As we have already said, particular (and largely Central European) disappointments lie behind these views as they were put forward in the Synod. But is it not true that there *had* to be so much talk of structural renewal because it was (and is) a question of overcoming outmoded mentalities? And are these renewed structures, which are in fact the expression and instrument of a living co-responsibility on the part of the community and the laypeople in it, *really* the reason why young people take a dislike to the institutional Church?

All the same, the Synod devoted a whole section of its report to a very fundamental statement on the Council's structural motif of 'communio', so here too a comparison is invited between this statement and those of the Council.

5. THE CHURCH AS 'COMMUNIO' IN THE CONCLUDING SYNOD REPORT

The concluding report describes the *'communio-ecclesiology as 'the central and fundamental idea of the Council documents'* (IIC1). This gives an important interpretation of the Council's statements on the Church and carries them further. For the relevant Council documents contain elements of a preconciliar juridical ecclesiology as well as elements of communio-ecclesiology. The difficulty in interpreting the Council's statements—which has been the cause of many conflicts in the Council's wake—is due precisely to this unrelated juxtaposition of the two ecclesiologies in the Council documents.[25] The same section also gives a very good presentation of the theological content and sacramental character of the communio-structure. While it properly enters a caveat lest the communio-ecclesiology be reduced to purely organisational questions concerning the exercise of power in the Church, it does resolutely underline the structural relevance of communio-ecclesiology: it constitutes 'the basis for order in the Church and in particular for the proper relationship which exists in it between unity and diversity' (IIC1).

By contrast, the following section on 'unity and diversity in the Church' contains surprisingly few creative new perspectives (IIC2). It stresses (indeed, like the Council documents) the unity of the whole Church, and warns of the danger of a false pluralism. We have not space to go into this in more detail here, but it must be pointed out that, unlike the Synod report, which sees the justification of diversity in unity only in the diversity of charisms and the multiplicity of the different parts of the Church, the Council also sees it in the multiplicity of 'the abilities, the resources and customs of peoples', so that 'each part contributes its own gifts to other parts and to the whole Church' (LG 13; cf. AG 4). In IIC2, however, as in the section on *enculturation* (IIDA), the openness with which the Council welcomed the enrichment of the Church through the multiplicity of cultures and situations has yielded to a certain reserve. The way the relationship between the whole Church and its parts is formulated also places the accent on the representation of the whole Church by the part, rather than on the way they mutually condition each other. Considering the developments and endeavours since the Council of the young churches in particular, as well as the statements of bishops' conferences and individual contributions at the Synod, it must be said that the concluding report is disappointing; in these matters the Council's perspectives were broader. The reason for this reticence is no doubt due less to those who compiled the report than to the fact that at the present time there are differing views, and the concluding report was trying to achieve the widest possible consensus.

It is to be welcomed that the concluding report sees collegiality as belonging to the doctrine of the Church as sacrament and as communio. '*Communio-ecclesiology provides the sacramental basis for collegiality*' (IIC4). By thus lifting collegiality out of a purely juridical perspective into a theological one, the report is able to describe the institutions of bishops' synods and bishops' conferences as 'various partial realisations' of collegiality, 'which are authentic signs and instruments of collegial awareness', and so guards against minimalist ideas of collegiality in the current debate.[26]

The structural relevance of communio-ecclesiology is also underlined in the section 'Participation and Co-responsibility in the Church': 'Since the Church is a communio, there must be participation and co-responsibility at all levels' (IIC6). What the Synod says in this section on 'the vocation and mission of women in the Church' has great practical application at the present time.

Finally the section 'Ecumenical Fellowship' similarly deduces the Church's ecumenical task from a sacramental and communio-ecclesiology (IIC7).

As far as this topic is concerned, therefore, the significant and positive result of the Synod is that the institutional side of the Church, and its structures, are consistently and systematically related to the motif of 'communio'. In this regard the conciliar teaching of the Church as mysterium-sacrament has proved decidedly fruitful. Indeed, the trinitarian and pneumatological dimension of the idea of *mysterium* and *communio* will need to be developed further so that, by developing the awareness and the structures of communio, and without anxiety, we can tackle the increasingly pressing problem of the Church's unity in growing diversity.[27]

Translated by Graham Harrison

Notes

1. See H. Stehle 'Die Flucht in das Mysterium' in *Die Zeit* no.50 (6.12.1985) p.11.
2. On 26.11.1985, reported in *L'Osservatore Romano*.
3. On 26.11.1985.
4. On 26.11.1985.
5. See J. Cardinal Ratzinger *Theologische Prinzipienlehre. Bausteine zur Fundamentaltheologie* (Munich 1982) p.388.
6. See the report of the German-speaking group, given on 3.12.1985, reported in *L'Osservatore Romano* (German Edition) no.51–52 (20.12.1985) p.9. Relevant in this connection are also the contributions of Cardinals Mayer (Congregation for the Sacraments), *ibid.*, p.7, and Simonis (Netherlands), *ibid.*, no.49, p.11.
7. On 27.11.1985, reported in *L'Osservatore Romano*.
8. On 26.11.1985, reported in *L'Osservatore Romano*.
9. See the concluding report of the Special Synod: *Herder Korrespondenz* 40 (1986) pp.40–48.
10. See H. J. Pottmeyer 'Vers une nouvelle phase de réception de Vatican II' in *La Recéption de Vatican II* ed. G. Alberigo/J.-P. Jossua (Paris 1985) p.47f.
11. See the Pope's add-ess at the concluding session on 7.12.1985: *L'Osservatore Romano*.
12. See L. Boff *Die Kirche als Sakrament im Horizont der Welterfahrung* (Paderborn 1972).
13. See *ibid.*, p.243.
14. See *ibid.*, pp. 229, 237f.
15. See W. Beinert 'Die Sakramentalität der Kirche im theologischen Gespräch' in *Theologische Berichte* IX (Einsiedeln 1980) p.13.
16. *See ibid.*, p.14f; P. Smulders 'Die Kirche als Sakrament des Heils' in *De Ecclesia. Beiträge zur Konstitution 'Über die Kirche' des Zweiten Vatikanischen Konzils.* ed. G. Baraúna (Freiburg 1966) pp.289–312.
17. L. Boff, the work cited in note 12, at p.274f.
18. *Constitutionis dogmaticae Lumen gentium synopsis historica* ed. G. Alberigo/F. Magistretti (Bologna 1975) p.436.
19. See in addition to L. Boff: W. Beinert, the work cited in note 15 at pp.13–66; M. Bernards 'Zur Lehre von der Kirche als Sakrament. Beobachtungen aus der Theologie des 19. und 20. Jahrhunderts' in *Münchner Theologische Zeitschrift* 20 (1969) pp.29–54.
20. See W. Beinert, p.24.
21. See L. Boff, pp.231, 243, 266.
22. L. Boff, p.257.
23. L. Boff, p.278.
24. L. Boff, p.536.
25. See H. J. Pottmeyer, the article cited in note 10, at pp.43–64.
26. See the editorial 'Il sinodo dei vescovi come sviluppo della collegialita episcopale' in *La Civiltà Cattolica* 136 (1985) fasc. 3248 pp.105–117.
27. See H. J. Pottmeyer 'Der eine Geist als Prinzip der Einheit der Kirche in Vielfalt' in *Pastoraltheologische Informationen* 5, 17th series (1986) fasc.2, p.253–284.

Henri Teissier

Bishops' Conferences and their Function in the Church

THE PURPOSE which the pope assigned to the 1985 Synod was, as is well known, an *evaluation of the reception of Vatican II* by the churches of five continents during the last twenty years. The work done by those attending did in fact develop around this central nucleus. Naturally the Synod's evaluation did not pay equal attention to all aspects of the Church's life since the end of the council. Certain topics dominated the discussions. The theme of *relations between individual churches and Rome occupied a decisive position.* Nevertheless, the angle of the question's direction varied in accordance with the person making the intervention. In Africa, for instance, it was raised especially in respect to enculturation. In Europe it was more a matter of balancing the distribution of tasks between the responsibility of diocesan bishops and that of the Roman dicasteries.

Very often the problem of relations between the individual churches and the Holy See was linked with that of the meaning and function of episcopal conferences in the present-day Church, their theological status should be 'given the value, indeed the necessity, of the pastoral work of bishops' conferences in the presen-day Church, their theological status should be examined so that in particular the question of their doctrinal authority could be explained more precisely and deeply' (II. C, 8).

1. THE TENOR OF THE SYNOD DISCUSSION IN REGARD TO CONFERENCES

It might be thought that this debate on the function of bishops' conferences raised only one relatively secondary question regarding the life of the Church.

It was only a matter, so it seems, of a division of tasks in the Church: between the pope and the Roman dicasteries on the one hand, and the diocesan bishops in their national, regional or continental groupings on the other hand. Seen thus, the discussion would hardly merit attention. In fact, the affirmation of the role of episcopal conferences, or the questioning of their role, *conceals a more important question.* This is nothing less than the *Church's unity, catholicity and loyalty to its mission.* It would be quite wrong to think, for instance, that the existing tension arose from the fact that the pope and Roman dicasteries controlled the unity of the Church, whereas the bishops controlled the specific mission of each individual church. To be sure, the pope is primarily responsible for the unity of the Church. But he does not bear that responsibility alone. The entire college of bishops, in communion with the pope—and never without him—also has the duty of ensuring and increasing the unity of the Church: 'The Church which as a whole is one . . . forms only one whole linked by the union of bishops' (Cyprian, letter 76: 8, 3). The bishops of individual churches, alone, or grouped together in conferences (national or regional) undoubtedly have the responsibility of preserving the loyalty of individual churches to their own mission. But they are not alone in carrying out that mission. The pope and the Roman dicasteries also have the duty of maintaining and serving the mission of each individual national, regional or continental church.

The same is true of the catholicity of the Church. Without the pope's ministry, the individual churches might become a scatter of national churches. But without the actual existence of individual churches in each country, region or continent, there would be no catholicity.

Hence the problem of relations between the bishops' conferences and the Petrine ministry is *not primarily a matter of a division of powers.* It has to be seen in the much wider perspective of the Church's loyalty to three of its decisive aspects: *unity, catholicity and mission.* In the context of this broader understanding of the problem, I should like to proffer the main lines of a reply to the wish expressed in the final Synod report, by indicating one of the appropriate directions for theological reflection on the exact function of episcopal conferences in the Church today.

2. CONSULTATION BETWEEN NEIGHBOURING BISHOPS, AND TRADITION

As is known, Cardinal Ratzinger stated in an interview 'that bishops' conferences have no theological foundation'.[1] This is obviously a recent and contingent ecclesial structure. Moreover, before tackling my topic directly, it seems appropriate to remind ourselves with a few examples that consultation among neighbouring bishops is quite traditional. In his book on individual churches in the universal Church,[2] Fr de Lubac notes that the development of so to speak 'church families', before becoming a socio-cultural phenomenon (churches of one nation or a single language) is linked first with the history of their evangelisation.

Since consultation between neighbouring Eastern churches is a well known phenomenon, its importance has to be shown in the Latin Church, starting with the situation of the bishops who recognised the primacy of Carthage even though that city never laid claim to a patriarchal title. Cyprian's letters contain many testimonies to the importance as he saw it of communion between the bishops of his region. I should like to refer, however, to the *long episcopate of Aurelius of Carthage*, since it is a period that is particularly well known. We can follow over a period of thirty years the interrupted succession of general or provincial councils which established busy relations between the Proconsular bishops (northern Tunisia), and those of Byzacena (Southern Tunisia), Numidia (Constantinian), Tripolitania (Libya), and Setifian, Caesarean (Algerian) and Tingitanian (Moroccan) Mauretania. The regularity of meetings between bishops corresponds to the experience of an episcopal conference today. One difference is that the duration of absences in the period shows how important the bishops thought these African church councils were.

Between 393 and 427, under the episcopate of Aurelius of Carthage, there would seem to have been some twenty general councils for 'all Africa'. These general sessions should be supplemented by five Pro-consular councils (Northern Tunisia). We also know in the same period of two provincial councils in Byzacena, without counting meetings such as the famous 411 assembly at Carthage, which was not called a 'general council for Africa' but nevertheless brought together some 280 Catholic bishops and as many Donatist bishops.[3]

All these links between bishops of neighbouring churches, within the framework of the historical patriarchates of the East (see LB 23 and CD 36), or within that of a regional church (continental in the sense of the age) like that for Roman Africa, expressed a deep-lying conviction that *the bishop could do his duty only in communion with the college of bishops*, beginning with the pastors of those churches which were closest geographically and culturally. Clearly the institution of episcopal conferences was contingent. It is a mode of organisation of communion, like *ad limina* visits or the pope's pastoral trips. But beyond this contingent structure we must acknowledge the existence of a *theological reality* which is part of the very nature of the Church, whose universal communion depends, to a great degree, on communion between bishops. Even in the third century St Cyprian wrote: 'There is reason for the existence of a numerous episcopal body all of whose members are united by the bond of mutual feelings of concord: the reason is that if any member of our college tried to strike out on his own and to split Christ's flock, the others would come to his help and return the (lost) sheep of the Lord to the flock' (Letter 78: III, 27). Studies of this topic which deserve support after the Synod should demonstrate the various forms of communion which ensured the unity of the episcopal body over the centuries, and thus provided the present institution of episcopal conferences with its basis as a service of unity and communion of the apostolic college.

3. BISHOPS' CONFERENCES AND COLLEGIALITY

All the foregoing is in fact closely connected with the discussion of collegiality and its putting into effect through bishops' conferences. Vatican II revealed clearly the constant belief of the Church that 'the bishops exercise (their episcopal charge)—in regard to the *magisterium* and government—on behalf of the universal Church of God, all united in a college or body, in communion with the Sovereign Pontiff and under his authority' (CD 3). Consequently, as *Lumen Gentium* says, 'Together with their head, the Supreme Pontiff, and never apart from him, (the order of bishops) have supreme and full authority over the universal Church' (LG 22). Episcopal collegiality therefore extends, in the first instance, from the basis of the care of all the bishops, in communion with the pope, for the universal Church. Should we see the work of the bishops' conferences as *a means of putting into effect this universal pastorate*, taking into account the fact that it concerns only the bishops of one country or one region, and does not directly engage the pope? The latest document of the International Theological Commission does not think so and talks, in regard to conferences, of the putting into effect of what it calls 'collegial feeling' (*affectus collegialis*).[4] The final Synod report treats this question in a similar perspective, but formulates it more broadly. It recognises 'that strictly speaking collegial action implies the activity of the college as a whole, together with its head, on all the Church' (II. C, 4). But, the report adds, there are 'partial instances of this collegial spirit such as the synod of bishops, bishops' conferences, the Roman Curia, *ad limina* visits (*ibid.*)'. I think that this way of looking at things limits excessively the conditions for exercising collegiality, which then to all intents and purposes would no longer exist apart from ecumenical councils. In fact there are other forms of the exercise of the universal pastorate of bishops which deserve review. They depend especially on bishops coming together in conference. Quite often, for instance, the universal episcopate is consulted by a Roman dicastery, at the pope's request, through the mediation of bishops' conferences. This is the case in particular in respect of replies requested from conferences when episcopal synods are held. It is also the case in regard to the preparation of more important documents, as it was for instance for the new code. John-Paul II himself has referred to 'collegiality' in respect of conferences, for instance, as Fr Dulles points out, at the Brazilian bishops' conference in the summer of 1980. He said that in that conference he recognised 'a noteworthy expression and a particularly appropriate organ of collegiality'.[5]

But one should never become a prisoner of words. If it seems desirable, the term 'collegial' may be reserved for ecumenical councils. But clearly customary participation of bishops in the cares of the universal Church occurs to a considerable extent nowadays through the medium of conferences, even if other forms of exercising this responsibility can and should exist.

4. INDIVIDUAL CHURCHES AND EPISCOPAL CONFERENCES

Another question which needs some light from theological research after the Synod is that of the *relations between the conference and each individual bishop*. As is known, Cardinal Ratzinger also posed this question forcefully in his theological interview. 'The valuation of the bishop's role at Vatican II was actually attenuated, even risking being squashed altogether by the integration of bishops into increasingly organised episcopal conferences.' Obviously the episcopal function is part of the 'essential structure' of the Church, to use the expression employed by the International Theological Commission. But it is just as obvious that the bishop cannot exercise his mission apart from full membership of the universal communion of bishops. Here there is a necessary and finely judged *play between the duty of communion with the other bishops and that of a permanent responsibility of pronouncing the Gospel*, if necessary with a discourse which, like that of the prophets, may have to be solitary for a certain time. The final Synod report reminds us that conferences should respect 'the inalienable responsibility of each bishop in respect of the universal Church and of his own individual church' (II. C, 5). Of course there is the danger of conferences overwhelming the responsibilities proper to each bishop, like the danger which also exists of Roman dicasteries intervening indiscreetly in diocesan affairs. But we must also consider the other possibility: that where a bishop's responsibility in regard to his mission demands of him united action with the neighbouring churches to produce common activity and discourse. Today there is a host of questions which can be answered only by a collective effort at the level of an ecclesiastical province, national or regional conference, or continental structure. Archbishop Malone expressed this aspect of things very appropriately in 1984 before the US bishops' conference which he was chairing, and did so by maintaining that a good example of the way in which a conference adds something to the personal role of a bishop is the capacity to take a decision, through the mediation of the conference, on questions of national scope and interest (DC 3.2.85). That is in fact the first reason cited by *Christus Dominus* to explain the necessity of conferences (CD 37).

'Above all in our times, it is not rare for bishops to be unable to carry out their duties appropriately and fruitfully, if they do not effect together with other bishops a form of cooperation which grows closer each day and a more coordinated form of action . . . Moreover the council thinks it quite opportune that in all places the bishops of one nation or of the same region should constitute a single assembly and that they should come together on fixed days in order to share with one another the lessons of their prudent experience' (no. 37).

There is also a need to advance thought about the bond between the communion of individual churches with one another and that of the bishops with one another in accordance with the ideas of, for example, Fr Legrand in his study of the Church's realisation in a locality.[6]

5.   THE DOCTRINAL AUTHORITY OF CONFERENCES

The final Synod report also asks that there should be an analysis of 'the question of doctrinal authority' of conferences, which was put in question, as is well known, by Cardinal Ratzinger's interview. Fr Dulles, in the above mentioned article, reminds us that in principle this question was already adumbrated by canon 753 of the new code, which states: 'Bishops separately or together in conferences or in individual councils, though they do not enjoy infallibility when teaching, are the authentic doctors and masters of the faith of the faithful confided to their care'. We see that this text aligns the teaching of the bishop in his own diocese and that of bishops together in special councils or an episcopal conference.

It might be objected that teaching in conference has no value in each individual diocese, where anyway it is the responsibility of the local bishop. But this statement does not prevent a teaching presented by all the bishops together at a conference assuming a special value for all the faithful concerned. *The Church is communion and the manifestation of its doctrine in a wider communion gives its discourse a very special weight*. That is precisely one of the *raisons d'être* of councils, which, as has been said, are 'events of churches' where the common discourse of the bishops may take up, in particular though not uniquely, some challenge of the moment which has to do with loyalty to faith.

The final Synod report states that 'in episcopal conferences the bishops of one nation or of the same territory exercise their pastoral duty conjointly' (II.C, 5). This may not exclude one of the main dimensions of their ministry, which is that of teaching the doctrine of faith. To support this finding, we may like Fr Dulles have recourse to statements of John-Paul II, for instance in the apostolic exhortation *Reconciliatio et Penitencia* (2.12.84): in regard to the Church's teaching in the social domain, the pope cites especially 'the teaching of various episcopates asked to intervene in different circumstances encountered in their countires' (RP 26).

On the disciplinary level, the new code (can. 455) has provided for conditions in which conferences could pass general decrees (cf. CDD, D, 38, 4). There is no limitation to teaching in common, which anyway has become an increasingly important reality in the life of many national or regional churches. In his speech of presentation of the statement of the US bishops on economic questions, Archbishop Malone has already suggested principles of interpretation for such teaching which ought to be taken into consideration (November 1984).

6. COMMUNION IN ACCORDANCE WITH MISSION

In conclusion, I should like to return to the main topics on the basis of which the final Synod report has been constructed: 'The ecclesiology of communion is the central and fundamental concept in the conciliar documents' (II. C, 1). The questioning by some of the part played by the bishops' conferences relies on certain excesses (bureaucracy and so forth), but cannot quarrel with the significance of this *structure of communion intended by the council*, recognised by the code, and made necessary even by the sheer growth of the Church over a century. Even in the third century, Cyprian of Carthage referred the dual dimension of communion without which there would be no Catholic Church: communion with the Church of Rome and communion between neighbouring churches. Hence in the case of the '*lapsi*', writing to the priests of Rome he told them that he intended 'to join company with several bishops [of Africa], and, not without agreeing with you [of Rome], to regulate and reform everything' (Letter 20, III, 3).

The organisation of the Latin Church for several centuries in the reduced form of a Western patriarchate is henceforth null and void. As a result of the missionary zeal which the popes and Roman dicasteries have in fact always maintained, the churches are now alive in the five continents. The structures of communion may change but the Church is truly Catholic only when it can experience at the same time a deepening of its unity and an extension of its mission. On the one hand, the unification of the world makes the worldwide unity of the Catholic Church more significant than ever before. On the other hand, the variety of cultural and socio-political situations implies a considerable effort to ensure enculturation and implantment of the Gospel at a level beyond the powers of isolated dioceses. Episcopal conferences, like synods, patriarchates, the pope's pastoral visits, and so forth, serve this dual purpose. If, in order to allow their bond with Rome a privileged status, the three thousand dioceses of the world were left without any form of interrelation, that would close the door to ecumenism, destroy the Catholic notion of unity, and totally annihilate the evangelical thrust of mission.

Translated by J.G. Cumming

Notes

1. J. Ratzinger and V. Messori *Entretien sur la foi* (Fayard 1985) p. 67
2. H. de Lubac (Aubier 1971) p. 47
3. André Mandouze gives a table of these councils and data in *Prosopographie chrétienne du bas Empire, Afrique* (Paris 1982) pp. 1318-1320. From the time of Cyprian onwards councils were held twice a year, in spring and autumn, in Carthage: see V. Saxer *Saints anciens d'afrique du Nord* (Rome 1979) p. 64
4. The International Theological Commission *L'Eglise dans le monde* (*Documentation Catholique* No. 1909 p. 65.
5. Avery Dulles 'Bishops' Conference documents, What doctrinal authority?' *Origins* 85 No. 32 (Jan. 85) 530. For a use of collegiality in connection with episcopal conferences in the discourses of John Paul II to the bishops of New Guinea, see *Documentation Catholique* 1876 p. 626. And for a development, see the discourse to the Swiss bishops in *Documentation Catholique* 1878 pp. 734-735. The most complete recent study on our theme to my knowledge is that of Mgr Bernard Franck 'La Conférence épiscopale et les autres institutions de collégialite intermédiaire' in *L'Année canonique* XXVII (1983) 67-120. The limits of this article do not allow me to substantiate the point but it seems to me that the article adduces important arguments in support of the point of view advanced here.
6. Hervé Legrand in *Initiation à la pratique de la théologie* (Paris 1983) pp. 144-180.

Peter Huizing

Subsidiarity

THE FINAL report of the Extraordinary Synod of Bishops in 1985 contained in Section C 'The Church as a Community' (*Communio*), n. 8, c, the following remarkable recommendation: 'It is recommended that an investigation should be conducted into the question as to whether the principle of subsidiarity that applies to human society is also applicable within the Church and, if so, to what extent and in what sense it can be applied and is possibly necessary (see Pius XII, *ASS* 38, 1946, p. 144)'.

This recommendation is above all remarkable because it is *in complete contradiction to the text of Pius XII to which it refers*. In other words, it is diametrically opposed to what the pope said to the recently appointed members of the College of Cardinals on 20 February 1946 on the occasion of the internationalisation of the College. The pope took as his point of departure Paul's outline given to the Christian community at Ephesus of the building up of the Church on the basis of different gifts given by the Lord to the faithful to equip the 'saints' for their 'work of service, building up the body of Christ' (Eph 4:11–16). He then quoted from the Encyclical *Quadragesimo Anno* promulgated by Pius XI on 15 May 1931, in which it is stated that it is in conflict with God's law to withdraw from man what he can achieve individually with his own efforts and his own plans and hand it over to the community. Pius XII applied this directly to the relationship between smaller and lower and bigger and higher communities. He then continued with the quotation from *Quadragesimo Anno*: 'All the activity of the community is by virtue of its being and conception subsidiary. It has the task of supporting the members of the community, but should not annihilate it or swallow it up.' Finally, Pius XII himself explained that this principle applied to all branches of social life, including the life of the Church, without injury to its hierarchical structure.

It is clear from the pope's address to the Second World Congress on the Lay

Apostolate on 5 October 1957 that he did not intend this addition to be interpreted as a restriction in the sense of 'on condition that it does not harm its hierarchical structure'. In that address, he explained that the authority of the Church has to apply the principle of subsidiarity with regard to the lay apostolate, in other words, that the laity has to be entrusted with the tasks that it can carry out as well as or even better than priests. Lay people must be able to act freely and accept responsibility within the limits of their particular task and that which is placed before them by the universal importance of the Church.[1] This principle of subsidiarity was, for Pius XII, *a fundamental norm of justice both for the hierarchical authority of the Church and for the order that had to be maintained by that authority.*

But there are further reasons for regarding the recommendation of the 1985 Synod as very remarkable. One reason is that it does not agree at all with the *judgment of the First Universal Assembly of the Synod of Bishops* that was held in 1967 shortly after the Second Vatican Council with regard to the principle of subsidiarity in the government of the Church. A number of principles were submitted to that Synod for the bishops to assess in connection with the revision of the Code of Canon Law. These principles had been suggested by the Papal Commission that had been appointed to revise the Code and compose with the explicit intention of establishing *general guidelines* so that the principles themselves and the spirit of the Council would be felt in the revised Code.

Principle No. 4 was entitled: 'The Inclusion of Special Powers in the Code', but it implied more than this. Until then, the diocesan bishops had asked Rome about all kinds of matters—some of them quite senseless—or received special powers from Rome for them. The conciliar decision concerning the pastoral task of the bishops (No. 8) laid down that diocesan bishops, as the successors of the apostles (!), would in future have, by virtue of their office, direct authority in their own dioceses to be exercised on their own responsibility. That competence would include the authority that was required for the exercise of their pastoral office, but it would not include the authority of the popes to reserve certain clearly defined cases for themselves or for other authoritative bodies. The diocesan bishops also obtained the authority to exempt believers for whom they had direct care in exceptional cases from having to observe the universal law of the Church, if they regarded that as something that was in the interest of their spiritual well-being. This power was given to the bishops also with the exception of certain clearly defined cases that were reserved to Rome.

The question of these reserved cases was once again discussed in Principle No. 5, as part of the wider theme of the 'application of the principle of subsidiarity in the Church'. Another way of applying this principle was used in the Council. This consisted of drawing up universal norms and allowing sufficient freedom for them to be *adapted to local needs by local procedures*. The management of Church property and possessions, for example, was in future to be to a great extent conducted in accordance with national customs and laws. One form of jurisdiction was required by the Church's procedural law, for example, but this had to be adapted to the norms that applied locally in the case of legal procedure.

When the Synod came to vote, Principle No. 4 was passed with 139 votes for, 2 against and 46 for 'subject to certain reservations'. But these 'reservations' either placed emphasis on certain points or else insisted on the principle of subsidiarity being applied also to religious and to persons who were competent to act legally in the Church, so that these might be given greater independence. Principle No. 5 was approved with 128 votes for, only 1 against and 38 for 'subject to certain reservations'. In this case the 'reservations' were either that the norms for a correct application of the principle should be clearly defined or that the principle should be extended to all branches of the Church's life, including the laity, although one voter regarded that as wrong and dangerous.[2]

It would take too long to examine the applications of this principle in the Code of Canon Law of 1983. In any case, it has certainly *been accepted in the Church's legislation and is practised there*. Perhaps the most striking example is that local churches, dioceses, parishes and religious communities are no longer seen as administrative parts of one single world Church, but rather as *independent subjects of the Church's life and law* and as communities in which and from which the one Church exists.

In the First Extraordinary Assembly of the 1969 Synod of Bishops, Paul VI referred to the principle of subsidiarity, which, even when the Synod was being prepared, many bishops had presented as an important norm in the relationship between the people and those bearing office in the Church and between the pope and the bishops. Pope Paul VI stressed in his address that this principle should be applied carefully without jeopardising the general well-being of the Church through the existence of too widely different and too far-reaching forms of autonomy in local churches. But even in that Synod, there was no doubt at all that the principle had to be applied.[3]

What was the situation in the 1985 Synod? The report of the replies made by the conferences of bishops to the questions asked by the Secretariat of the Synod, a document that was published by Cardinal Danneels, disclosed that many of the respondents wanted an *improvement in the relationship between the local churches and the Roman Curia*. Special attention was also given to the collegiality of bishops and to the function of episcopal conferences in Cardinal Danneels' document and these themes were discussed again and again in the Synod itself. Bishop James W. Mallone, the president of the United States bishops' conference, expressed the wish that the doctrine of Vatican II concerning collegiality and the impulse that the various conferences had been given by that doctrine should be reinforced. The ex-bishop of Oslo, John Gran, who was representing the Norwegian conference of bishops, called for a more efficient practical application of the principle of subsidiarity—the tendency towards a return to the idea of diocesan bishops acting more as representatives of Rome than as independent leaders ought not to be underestimated. Archbishop Carter of Kingston, Jamaica, complained that many decisions that ought to be taken in dioceses were in fact still taken in Rome. The president of the Australian bishops' conference, Archbishop Francis Robert Rush, pleaded for a careful theological foundation and a more efficient functioning of bishops' conferences.[4] It would seem that none of the participants in the Synod felt any need to call the principle of subsidiarity into question. On the contrary, they all appeared to accept it. *Why, then, was the recommendation made to examine the application of the principle?*

A report made by *Peter Hebblethwaite*, who was described by one of his colleagues as a 'top Vaticanist', may perhaps contain a clue to this.[5] One of the bishops had suggested to the assembly that a great deal of trouble might have resulted from the application of the principle of subsidiarity in the question of the theology of liberation, in other words, if the authority of the local church—in this case, the church of Brazil—had been recognised. Two Brazilian prelates, José Ivo Lorscheiter and Aloisio Lorscheider, had submitted their judgment of this theology in writing to the Synod. The Columbian Bishop Dario Castrillon Hoyos had attacked this theology and the 'people's Church' very violently in public. Hebblethwaite's conclusion was that this threw a sharp light on the *conflict between those who wanted real collegiality and those who wanted centralisation.*

According to a press communiqué published on 22 November 1985, *Jean Hamer* had spoken in the meeting of the College of Cardinals before the Synod about the relationship between the Roman Curia and the diocesan bishops and their conferences. After having emphasised the ecclesiological significance of the Curia, he went on to deal especially with the nature of the bishops' conferences and the appeal to the principle of subsidiarity.

Hamer apparently argued that the distinctive characteristic of the Curia is that it supports the pope in his highest pastoral function, but does not support the College of Bishops as such, even though the latter shares this function together with the pope, in view of the fact that the Curia receives its existence and its authorities from the head and not from the College. Nonetheless, the Curia is guided by the same pastoral care which unites the head and the members of the same College in the same service of the Church. Hence the

Curia has the task of being connected with all churches and the latter have the right and the duty to be connected with the Curia. The bishops' conferences are not local forms of the College of Bishops, but assemblies of local bishops with no more authority than that which they possess as such. In cases determined by papal right or mandate in which they are able to make collegially binding decisions, the obligation rests with the authority of the pope, not with that of the bishops.

Finally, Hamer put forward the following arguments against the principle of subsidiarity. It is generally applied within the framework of political society, including pronouncements by the Church about this. In the Church, it is sufficient to respect the competence of the local Church. Many people believe that the principle retains its political characteristics. It attributes a subsidiary function to the universal Church with regard to the local church and the universal Church has a task that is not merely subsidiary.

So much, then, for the reports about Hamer's arguments presented to the Cardinals. With the reports about the Synod in mind, it is difficult to avoid seeing a *link between Hamer's arguments*, which form the only plea against the principle of subsidiarity, *and the recommendation made by the Synod*, the background to which was presumably the tensions that had formed around the theology of liberation and had in this case been concentrated on the question of competence, the question, in other words, as to who has the last word. Hence a theology of the Roman Curia as an organ of the universal Church, a theology of bishops' conferences as councils of individual diocesan and other bishops which remain free and independent but can exercise a legally binding authority only by virtue of the 'authority of the universal Church' and which above all possess no teaching authority. Hence also the replacement of the principle of subsidiarity by a recognition of the competence legally attributed to the local churches.

Without going any further into this 'ecclesiology' as a 'theology of the Church' consisting of theologising or declaring as theologically valid the existing law of the Church, it has to be pointed out in this context that the *special and indeed theological significance of the principle of subsidiarity in the Church community is lost in this construction*. Even more than in civil or political society, care has to be taken in the community of the Church that the meaning and implication of pastoral guidance and the regulations that have to be supplied to meet this need consist not in the maintenance of an external public order, but in supporting and encouraging personal experiences of Christian faith and personal participation in the life of the Church community. The 'hierarchical structure' has an original Christian destiny that is completely at the service of this. It is in this much more complete sense what Pius XI called 'by virtue of its being and conception subsidiary'.

Translated by David Smith

Notes

1. *AAS* 39 (1957), 922–939, especially 927.
2. *Communicationes* 1 (1969), 80–82, 89, 96, 99f.
3. *Herder Korrespondéz* 23 (1969), 535.
4. *Ibid.* 40 (1986), 36.
5. 'Extraordinary Synod' in *Streven* 53 (1986) 435–448.

The following articles are relevant: W. Bertrams 'De principio subsidiarietatis in iure canonico' *Periodica de re morali*... 46 (1957) 13–65; M. Kaiser 'Das Prinzip der Subsidiarität in der Verfassung der Kirche' *AKathKR* 133 (1964), 3–13; F. Klüber 'Soziallehre' *LThK* 9 917–920; René Metz 'La Subsidiarité, principe régulateur des tensions dans l'Eglise' *RDC* 22 (1972) 155–176; 'De principio subsidiarietatis in iure canonico' *Acta conventus internationalis Canonistarum Romae diebus 20–25 maii 1968 celebrati* (Vatican 1970), 297–306; O. von Nell-Brüning 'Subsidiarität in der Kirche' *StZ* 204, 111 (1986) 147–156.

Jacques Gaillot

Opting for the Poor

THE SYNOD speaks of a bias towards the poor. That in itself is an event. What was already an established fact in Latin America is extending over the whole world-wide Church. What was declared at Medellin and Puebla has now, through the Synod, reached a world-wide audience. This famous notion is destined to become *part of the common heritage of the Catholic Church.*

At what point in its message does the Synod speak of this bias towards the poor? Right at the end. And that too is illuminating. After dealing with the mystery of the Church, the sources of the Church's life, and the Church as communion, the final report turns to the mission of the Church in the world. It underlines the importance of the constitution *Gaudium et Spes*, notes the central place of the theology of the cross, spells out what is involved in an authentic *aggiornamento*, mentions the difficult problem of enculturation, and re-opens the dialogue with non-Christian religions and with unbelievers. It then ends the series with the 'bias towards the poor and human development'. 'Since Vatican II the Church has become more conscious of its mission to be at the service of the poor, the oppressed, the marginalised. On this bias, which must not be regarded as exclusive, shines the true spirit of the Gospel. Jesus Christ said "Blessed are the poor", and himself chose to be poor among us.'

The Synod extended the scope of the bias towards the poor. 'In addition to material poverty, there is the lack of liberty and of spiritual assets, which may be regarded as a form of poverty. This lack is particularly serious where religious liberty is suppressed by force.

'The Church must speak prophetically in denouncing every form of poverty and oppression. It must defend and promote in every place the fundamental and inalienable rights of the human person.'

Those are the strong words which require us to take seriously the cause of the poor. But is this not just one more statement about the poor? There is, it is true, no shortage of totally ineffective statements about the various forms of poverty. Twenty years on from the Council, we might well ask what has happened to the famous theme of the servant Church and the poor Church! These few pages are not intended as just another statement about the poor, but as the simple testimony of a pastor who is trying to be the Church with the poor, and who knows that in this area above all, actions are indispensable. People look for action from the Church.

1.   WHO ARE THE POOR IN THE DIOCESE OF EVREUX?

Before trying to answer the question and identify the poor, we must take note of some *difficulties*:-

Annoyance caused by the word. When the word 'poor' is mentioned in a meeting, it produces the annoyed reaction: 'Don't use that word which means too much and yet means nothing. Are we not all poor in some respect? There is not only material poverty.' In the course of a meeting to prepare a Christmas vigil for the most deprived people in the town, the fateful word was used. Immediately a priest interposed: 'Please let us not use this word, which is always being bandied about.' The word was not spoken again throughout the entire evening. We were preparing Christmas for those whose name we were no longer able to utter.

Marginality. We cannot fail to realise that the poor are not regular clients of the Church. They are not part of the institution, but the institution tries to concern itself with them. Christians who get involved with the poor risk becoming marginalised themselves in relation to the institution.

Danger of establishment. Must it not be recognised that wherever the Church sets itself up it develops a 'rich' mentality? Is it not a fact that the Church produces Christians who settle down and become conservative? The Church has its poor, and institutions which take account of that fact. There are Christians who practise individual poverty, but they share in the collective wealth of our country.

Accusation of Communism. To take the side of the poor is to be accused of being Communist. How does it happen that people are accused of Communism when they get involved with the poor? There are Catholics for whom this confidence placed in the poor is unacceptable.

What project of liberation? For what purpose do we want a Church of the poor? It is not a question of canonising the poor. In the Gospel, Jesus has a mobilising project: to declare to prisoners that they are free, and to the blind that they will see the light; to bring liberation to the oppressed . . . .

In Latin America, whether it be Brazil, Chile, Guatemala or Nicaragua, a project of liberation can energise a whole people. But here in France, in a society gradually coming under the influence of information technology, it is more difficult to promote liberation. Who are the poor? They are always subjugated, the oppressed. They constitute basic poverty. Let us beware of idealising poverty.

As in biblical times God never ceases to take the side of the oppressed. He cannot accept the injustice done to them. He takes care of them. He comes close to them.

In the diocese of Evreux, the poor can be identified as the young unemployed and the immigrants. They know economic poverty and the poverty of being at risk. For them the horizon is closed. They find that they have no future. The poor are also identified as prisoners, and patients in the psychiatric hospital. They are deprived of liberty and tenderness. Some of them do not exist for anybody. Nobody is waiting for them. Nobody visits them. Nobody loves them. They live in isolation, shut up in their solitude. The poor are also identified as families in rented accommodation who have had their electricity cut off because they cannot pay. These families know material poverty, everyday poverty.

The list could be extended still further. Let me now give some indication of the action being taken to apply this bias towards the poor.

2. WHAT ACTIONS ARE BEING TAKEN?

The bias towards the poor is expressed modestly in a life-style, in choices made and initiatives taken, in association with non-Christians. The path is a difficult one, along which we have to feel our way. Losing its traditional supports and its ancient privileges is a source of purification for the Church. The following are some of the actions which mark out the way.

Solidarity with immigrants. Immigrants are up against racism daily, in this time of economic crisis. Along with many others, I have denounced racism as an insult to man, to his dignity and to his rights. It is impossible to support human rights and have a racist attitude. Thus I have been led to give evidence in court on behalf of an immigrant from Zaire, to affirm my solidarity with hunger-strikers from the same country, and to declare on television that I was in favour of votes for immigrants on the occasion of the municipal elections.

More important are the bonds which are formed daily between those who live round the same stair-well in rented accommodation. Thus when a hemiplegic Moroccan mother is unable to take her children to nursery school, the other mothers in the block get together and see to it that the children can go regularly to school. The mother is grateful, and the father can go to work with peace of mind.

Other signs of hope for the future are to be seen in the simple and natural bonds being formed between parishes and immigrants. Immigrants are sharing in pastoral committees, in catechesis, in preparation for baptism, in worship, in youth groups.

Such signs as these are helping to give a new image to the Church. But, in relation to immigrants, some questions remain: shall we be able to make the transition from being a Church which accepts immigrants to being a Church which lives with them? There are some small, well-established religious communities which are inviting us to make this transition. Shall we be able to allow immigrants to have a full say in the affairs of the Church?

The action of the C.C.F.D. If there is one place where most of the living forces in the Church today are to be found, it is the C.C.F.D. (Comité Catholique contre la Faim et pour le Développement—Catholic Committee against Hunger and for Development). Right away this Committee turns the attention of the Church in our diocese towards the Third World, with the object of promoting development along with the Third World, and not simply for it. The C.C.F.D. helps people to understand that development is not simply economic. It is cultural. Therefore it is necessary to create a dynamic of sharing of solidarity, of respect for everyone's rights, so that there can be true partnership. This year the C.C.F.D. has a Lent campaign in six parts of the diocese, with five projects, involving Afghanistan, Benin, Bolivia, Mexico and Thailand.

The problems of the Third World are not marginal to our own problems. The Third World invites us to act at home to fight the causes of under-development.

Today, as yesterday, the Kingdom of God is present where the poor are hearing the Good News. A Church which is tied to the powerful and the privileged is incapable of proclaiming the Good News. Is not the C.C.F.D. reminding us that the Church is never so much alive as when it is looking beyond its own frontiers?

Money: a test for the Church in the diocese. When we speak of money, we are touching on the Church's life and the evidence for that life. We are checking how the Church is organised, and looking at the priorities which it sets itself. I am always hearing it said that the Church is rich. In spite of the financial difficulties in our diocese, people continue to believe that the Church is rich. That is a serious obstacle. Hence the importance of taking action, and of changing our life-style. It is a fact that we are living beyond our means. It is easier to talk about the Third World than to look at the way in which we manage our own financial affairs.

Speaking of money is not alien to the mission. Being clear and open about parochial and diocesan finances is a question of honesty. The money we receive is not ours. Reducing the inequalities which exist between those parishes which have few resources and those which have plenty is a question of justice. Taking steps to achieve greater solidarity is essential for the mission.

Those parochial finance committees which put their affairs in order are helping the movement towards greater clarity and solidarity. There is still a long way to go.

Will the Church in the diocese make some gestures of sharing? Will it discover a life-style inspired by the Gospel? Will it find ways to be poor for the sake of its mission?

Towards a pastoral practice based on kindness. Many people turn to the Church only when they want to avail themselves of the sacraments. Families regularly come to me and protest because they have been upset by the refusal of their request for a sacrament. I think of the lorry-driver, whose daughter had been refused marriage because there had not been the required three months of preparation. He said angrily: 'The Church has no heart—only concrete.' I think also of the night-shift worker who had been refused baptism for his child because, in that case also, the proper notice had not been given. He came to see me, and said: 'Everything has been arranged. We were looking forward to a family celebration. But I'm hitting my head against a brick wall. The Church is preventing us from celebrating.'

We could make a long list of those who have come up against the brick wall of the Church. Such people are not regular churchgoers. They know little of the life of the Church, and even less of its rules. Why lay such heavy burdens on them? The requirements which we lay down for the sacraments should be complied with first by those who produce them. Whatever barriers we may set up in the way of access to the sacraments, we should be careful that they are not stumbling-blocks to the poor.

When the poor knock loudly on the door of the Church, a word of Jesus comes to my mind: 'See that you do not despise any of my little ones' (Matt. 18:10). He who does not offer a welcome, cannot claim the support of the Gospel.

Deacons for a Church in solidarity with the poor. Deacons have been ordained to help the Church in the diocese to be ready for service. They stimulate the desire to serve in the manner of Christ. Here is a boon for the communities. When the Holy Spirit is welcomed and received, he transforms the one who receives him into a servant.

Who will deny that, in our Church, power takes precedence over service? Or that organisation is preferred to love? Or that the weight of custom stifles the breath of the Gospel?

The Church has need of deacons so that it may become a servant and poor, close at hand and readily accessible. That is why I continue to call for candidates for the diaconate, on the basis of felt needs, to encourage all members of the Church to engage in service. Might not the role of the Church be to offer disinterested service to mankind?

I am sure of this: whenever Christians rediscover care for the poor, something happens. The strength of Christians is in being joined with the poor.

A diocesan service of solidarity. The rapid changes taking place in our society are causing upheavals in all sectors of life. The crisis through which we are passing is not only an economic one. It is also a crisis of cultural identity. There is a profound sense of insecurity, which is expressed by:
—a withdrawal from the cold into small, warm human communities;
—a rapid decline in militancy;
—a return of the religious;
—a need for a scapegoat: the immigrants.
The Church is less and less present in those places where decisions are being put into effect, and where changes are taking place. There is a danger that the energies of the Church may be concentrated on problems of reorganisation related to the theme of co-responsibility. Hence the proposal for a diocesan service of solidarity, the aims of which are:
—*to put it on record* that a central pastoral preoccupation of the diocese is the presence of the Church alongside those most severely affected by the changes;
—*to put into effect*, in diocesan initiatives, in reflection, and in actions appropriate to the questions raised by the changes in our society, 'the Good News announced to the poor';
—*to recall* the ultimate missionary dimension in all that is being modified or adapted in the working of the communities and of the diocesan services.

This service of solidarity is composed of a dozen people from the various sectors of social life in which the new forms of poverty are being experienced, and in which new forms of solidarity are being tried out: unemployment, situations where delinquency is experienced, problems related to the presence of immigrants, social workers, psychiatry, people living in rented accommodation.

The Vicar General, who is the prison chaplain and the person responsible for the pastoral care of migrants, is the team leader.

Is it not a test of the health of the Church, whether it can witness beyond its own frontiers? And is not the impact which it can have outside its own structures a sign of its vitality?

Being the Church in the aftermath of Vatican II means starting from the circumference, and not from the centre. The renewal of the Church will come from its close links with the poor. That is true for the renewal of the ministry of priests and bishops. It is true for the mission of the laity. The power of the poor makes this renewal possible.

Translated by G.W.S. Knowles

Giuseppe Ruggieri

Open Questions: Church-World Relations

WHAT PROSPECTS did the Extraordinary Synod of 1985 open up for Church-world relations? In their final report the Synod fathers did not hesitate to put forward views differing from those of the Council, such as in their judgment of what they call 'secularism', or in the insinuation that *Gaudium et Spes* has to some extent been overtaken by events. (They recognise its value, but point out that the context of 'signs of the times' is now somewhat different: II.D.1). And, so as to justify their pessimistic view of the world and the twenty years that have passed since the end of the Council as characterised by 'secularism', they introduce this judgment with the observation that 'the short space of twenty years has brought about rapid changes in history' (II.A.1). This repeated appeal to changed historical conditions, together with the no less forceful acceptance of the conciliar message itself, which they proclaim unreservedly, provides a good indication of the message the bishops seem to be giving Christians: *the message of the Council is being re-thought in the new historical conditions*. This process of re-thinking means subjecting the 'signs of the times' to ever new analysis (II.D.7).

So in their view of the mission of the Church in the world, which is to make the Gospel ever more clearly understood and the activity of the Church ever more intense, *a growing dynamism is needed in the reading of history*, a dynamism able to keep up with the speed of change in history itself. The bishops put forward *four lines* along which further thought is needed 'yet again' in this ever-renewed reading of the 'signs of the times'. These are: (a) the *theology of the Cross* in preaching, the sacraments and the life of the Church; (b) the theology and praxis of *enculturation*, not just dialogue with other religions and non-believers; (c) the preferential *option for the poor*, and (d) the social teaching of the Church in regard to *human advancement* in 'ever new circumstances'. There is no escaping this repeated reminder of the way things have changed and the need for an approach dynamic enough to keep up with the process of change! So let us take up the challenge and try to put forward some thoughts on the prospects that have been opened up, going over the key themes of the Synod itself.

1. THE SIGNS OF THE TIMES

The invitation to read the signs of the times of course stems from John XXIII and was taken up by the second Vatican Council, especially in *Gaudium et Spes*. This invitation basically had a double purpose. In the first place it sought to go beyond the negative attitude that had dominated the Catholic Church's considerations of modern history. In his apostolic constitution convoking the second Vatican Council, Pope John XXIII deliberately went against this attitude, proclaiming that 'we make ours the recommendation of Jesus that one should know how to distinguish the "signs of the times" (Matt. 16: 4), and we seem to see now, in the midst of so much darkness, a few indications which augur well for the fate of the Church and of humanity'. This *positive valuation of history*, as the place for hope because of what it contains, was taken up again in his opening address to the Council, *'Gaudet mater ecclesia'*.[1] In the second place, this invitation was to abandon the *deductivist* approach and replace it with an *inductive* mentality, examining the facts themselves and drawing from them signs of coherence between the Gospel as believed and proclaimed and human desires.[2]

One therefore has to ask whether the changed historical conditions to which the Synod fathers so repeatedly refer justify the reading of the signs of our times which they sought to give (I.3; I.4; II. A. 1), which takes exactly the *opposite approach*. On this point it is interesting to take another look at the way they judge *'secularism'*. They contrast this cultural phenomenon with a 'return to the sacred', seen as a positive phenomenon which the Church should favour in opposition to the former and in order to offer people of our time the first inklings of faith. The explosive growth of religious sects is therefore seen by the Synod fathers as a challenge to the Church itself, calling it to display a sense of the sacred to a greater extent (II.A.1).

It was in quite another spirit that the *Council dealt with the question of atheism*,[3] and accordingly it looked to a meeting between the Church and its contemporaries along quite different lines. Not that it saw atheism as without blame, but *Gaudium et Spes* (21b) maintained that, 'conscious of how weighty are the questions which atheism raises, and motivated by love for all men (the Church) believes these questions ought to be examined seriously and more profoundly'. This 'serious and more profound' examination led the Council fathers to recognise the justification for so much criticism of religion in our time, simply because of the failures of Christians who 'conceal rather than reveal the authentic face of God and of religion' (*ibid.*, 19g). Faced with a phenomenon seen in this way, the Council did not propose a return to the sacred as a remedy, but the course of *sharing*: faced with members of the other great religions and those who were strangers to the idea of God, or who expressedly denied his existence, the Church, in order to be able to offer them the mystery of salvation, 'must become part of all these groups for the same motive which led Christ to bind himself, in virtue of his Incarnation, to the definite social and cultural conditions of those human beings among whom he dwelt' (*Ad Gentes*, 10). A sign of the times, that of contemporary atheism, is here read without ingenuousness, and certainly not with the apologetics of confrontation, but as a stimulus for the Church to renew itself and rethink its presence as a friend. So *opposing secular culture to sacred culture was far from the spirit of the Council.* The Council in fact used the term 'sacred' with very great reserve, confining it to the traditional usage in phrases like 'sacred liturgy', 'sacred Scriptures', 'sacred power', etc. There is no trace in the Council of an apologetic of 'the sacred'; its proposal was for the Church to share in all human situations, however ambiguous they might be. And any pastoral worker knows the obstacles, as opposed to the advantages, which a 'sacral' mentality places in the way of genuine assimilation of the Christian message, as opposed to sociological and purely traditional identification with it.

Calling for an ever renewed reading of the signs of the times to accord with ever changing conditions, following in the wake of the Council, must also mean *immersing ourselves in history* as the place where God calls to the Church itself, calling it to listen and not just to judge.

2. THE THEOLOGY OF THE CROSS

The Synod fathers several times suggest the 'theology of the Cross' as a 'cultural method'. While they sometimes see the life of the Church itself as being under the sign of the witness of the Crucified One (*Final Document*, II.A.2), or as dominated by the mystery of the Cross and the Resurrection, between the persecutions of the world and the consolations of God (II.A.3), at other times they put forward the theology of the Cross as the *key to understanding the relationships binding human history to the history of salvation.* They are not seeking to exclude *the* theology of the creation and the Incarnation (strangely identifying these two theologies and distinguishing them as a single whole from the theology of the cross), since this is presupposed (II.D.2). They are rather seeking to understand how integral salvation comes together in a *triple* movement: *acceptance* of human reality, *purification* of it, and *elevation* of it, both with respect to the *aggiornamento* of the Church, and with respect to enculturation (II.D.3, 4).

This statement certainly reveals one basic aspect of the Christian experience, but whenever this is absolutised and becomes exclusive, Christian understanding of history is itself precluded. And yet it must be said that the theology of the Incarnation contains an element of *kenosis* which places it closer to the theology of the Cross than to that of creation (see Phil. 2: 6–7). The Son of God 'emptied himself to assume the condition of a slave', becoming like us in all except sin. This is precisely how we come to know the glory of the Father, who exalted his Son who remained obedient even unto death on the Cross. The Cross carries on the logic of the Incarnation; it does not introduce a new element into it.

Deepening the theology of the Cross, as it is witnessed by those who set out to follow Christ and seek to imitate his form of presence in their own times, means abandoning any pretensions to cultural hegemony, even if exercised in the name of the Cross. The Cross is not a standard to be hoisted at the head of a historical movement, but a revelation of the foolishness of God which is wiser than the wisdom of men. Once the word of the Cross stands out stripped and pure, people can effectively examine the mystery of God in its reality and freed from their own preconceptions. But this involves abandoning any cultural 'ecclesiocentrism' and working for the world, with its 'sovereignties and powers', to come, through the Church, to know the 'comprehensive' wisdom of God (Eph. 3: 10, where this act of learning comes from 'all eternity', a manifestation coming direct from God himself). There is no need, that is, to reduce the Cross to a dialectical, almost Hegelian, process, in which a reality is taken on, denied and surpassed. This would undermine the very meaning of the Resurrection, which is an act through which the Father glorifies the Son and not the final stage in a dialectical process. And the world itself, in its totality, is the subject of the saving dialogue with God. The Church has the mission of presenting this world with the foolishness of the Cross in order that the logic of God's love may shine through, with his 'patience with all' (2 Pet. 3: 9), 'wanting nobody to be lost and everybody to be brought to change his ways'. It is right to say that cultures should change their ways. But this *'change of ways' is the very stuff of history*, upheld by the magnanimity of God, in which the power of the risen Christ, working through his Spirit, is at work, even outside the Church (cf GS, 38).

The Synod final document suffers from its failure to recognise this *presence of Christ working in human desires* and the eschatological view of evangelisation. It suffers too from its failure to make adequate use of perhaps the Council's strongest passage on Church-world relations: *Lumen Gentium* 8, calling on the Church to follow Christ's example by proclaiming 'humility and self-sacrifice, even by her own example'. It does not seem to be by accident that any reference to 'the Church of the poor' is missing from the document. While the 'preferential option for the poor' is properly and rightly upheld, there is insufficient reminder that the *poor*, for the Church, are not primarily people to be defended or helped, but *subjects who question the Church itself*, showing it the faces of those whom Jesus calls blessed because for such is the Kingdom of God. Faced with the poor, the Church is therefore called to 'change its ways' ever more to those of its Lord who made himself poor, and not to take up the reins of a historical movement.

3. ENCULTURATION, DIALOGUE AND SOCIAL TEACHING

The final document's view of enculturation and *aggiornamento* is dominated by an approach which, among other things, strongly stresses the *connection between the Gospel and the moral values that derive from it* (II.B.a.2). Besides the recall to the sense of the sacred, it is this stressing of the double task that, so to say, characterises the mission of the Church: 'transmission of the faith and of moral values', that most strikes the reader.

This inclusion of transmission of moral values, alongside the transmission of faith, at the very centre of the Church's mission in the world, should be read in the light of the *history of the last two centuries*. Faced with societies evolving in directions away from the Church, the *magisterium* laid stress on reference to the moral order on which any human society should be based, a moral order which only the Church was in a position to know fully. One has the strange impression that, in modern times, the Church has more often been preoccupied with presenting an ethical, humanist and social, message than with the witness of the Cross itself.[4]

We need to get to the heart of the problem. Clearly, the Church and all believers have the duty to manifest and loudly proclaim the evangelical judgment on this world. But the problem lies in knowing *in what name they judge the world*: whether in the name of a human wisdom, however great and worthy of respect, or in the name of the Cross of Him who was rich but made himself poor in order to enrich the world through his poverty. The final document rightly (II.D.6) refers to the 'prophetic way' in which Christians should intervene in the world.

But then we have to look beyond a view to which the Synod's final document seems to be indebted, at least to some extent. This view on the one hand stresses the question of human rights and values as the main reference point for the presence of the Church in the world. On the other hand, it is still concerned with safeguarding the Church's role as the world's guide in upholding these same rights and values. The Church claims the right to occupy this role on the grounds of the inherent weakness of these rights and values, once they become separated from the tutelage of Christian values. So enculturation, dialogue and recognition of values run the risk of becoming the latest, and most acceptable, way of repossessing a *'potestas'* which may not be the direct one of old or even an indirect one, but is still one based on a social consensus, one achieved more cleverly and through the means of 'immanence'.

The Synod set out to be a celebration of the Council, an unreserved welcoming of its message. At the same time, in view of changed historical circumstances, it thought it right to shift some accents in relation to the Council itself, at least in its final document. Perhaps it is not wholly realistic to see this document as a 'summary' of the Synod itself. It was rather one of the acts of *reception* of the Council which the bishops of the Catholic Church have constantly carried out over the last twenty years.

If we are to follow the guidelines set out by the bishops at the Synod, it is now our task to proceed along the avenues they have opened up, comparing them on the one hand with *the message of the Council* and on the other with the *new situation of human history*. This raises the following question: faced with the re-emergence of religious wants and the persistence of a secular culture at the same time, and faced with a new demand from society itself for a basis for moral values, should the Church take its place as one 'competitor' among those who claim to provide the answers to these demands, or should it rather imitate God's 'patience with all' and present the message of the Cross in all its purity, without changing it into one way of winning support, but rather raising it among the nations as the revelation of the depth of the Father's love?

Translated by Paul Burns

Notes

1. Apostolic Constitution *Humanae Salutis* of 25.12.1961, in *The Documents of Vatican II* ed. W. M. Abbott (New York & London 1966) p. 704; Opening Speech to the Council *'Gaudet mater ecclesia'* in *ibid.* pp. 710–19.
2. See M.-D. Chenu 'Les Signes du temps' in *NRTh* 97 (1965), 29–39; G. Ruggieri 'Fede e storia' in *IL Vaticano II e la chiesa* ed. G. Alberigo & J.-P. Jossua (Brescia 1985) pp. 127–58.

3. The terms 'secularism' and 'secularisation' are not found in the Council texts. Atheism is obviously a different phenomenon. For the Synod, atheism forms a part of 'secularism'.

4. M.-D. Chenu *La Doctrine sociale de l'Eglise comme idéologie* (Paris 1979). Chenu's interpretation of the 'social teaching' of the Church has been widely criticised, but in my view the criticisms have been verdicts rather than serious critical discussions.

Giuseppe Alberigo

New Balances in the Church since the Synod

FROM A procedural and structural viewpoint, the Extraordinary Synod of 1985 presents a good *many anomalies*. By which I mean that during both its period of preparation and its duration, unaccustomed and contradictory things were done, at least in comparison with the practice of earlier synods.

As many bishops' conferences pointed out in their preparatory reports, the time allowed between the Synod's convocation and its opening was particularly short, and the time allowed to the bishops was made even shorter, since three months elapsed between the pope's announcement and the secretary of state sending out the preliminary questionnaire. All this had the effect of *contracting the preliminary consultations*, and this when the Synod was not to be a 'single subject' one, as previous ones had been, but examine the state of reception of Vatican II and therefore the whole state of the Church as it approached the end of its second millenium.

Equally anomalous was the fact that the subject matter for the Synod was laid down by the despatch of a series of questions to the bishops' conferences from the permanent Secretariat of the Synod itself. These questions, set out in two series, of which only the first seemed to originate with the Secretariat itself, while the second appeared to have been added on the initiative of the Roman Congregations, struck many people as inspired by a *static vision of Vatican II and the life of the Church*—as the Swiss bishops' conference explicitly remarked[1]—and therefore prejudicially orientated toward a negative view of the situation of the Church, if not openly aimed at provoking alarmist replies.

No less strange was the way in which, once this questionnaire had been sent out, the permanent Secretariat of the Synod was removed from the centre of the later stages of preparation, a process of *marginalisation* culminating in the exclusion of several distinguished members from the list of those participating in the assembly itself.[2] Even more surprising than the fact of these exclusions in themselves was the *resulting leaderlessness* in the later stages of preparation, which went so far as produce an atmosphere of increasing disagreement and disquiet as the date for the opening of the Synod drew nearer and information was still not forthcoming.

A final anomaly was the *absence of a preparatory or working document*, which gave the impression that the subsequent development of discussions was completely unpredictable. This atmosphere of uncertainty was unexpectedly worsened by an intervention from the secretary of State—as surprising as it was peremptory—who, in early autumn, forbade the episcopal conferences to make the texts of their preparatory reports public or even to exchange them with one another.[3]

This emasculation of the preparatory processes was seen to be particularly worrying in that the months immediately preceding the Synod were enlivened by various attempts to put *pressure on public opinion*, both inside and outside the Church, stemming from the Congregation for the Doctrine of the Faith and ultimately from its head, *Cardinal Ratzinger*. This unusual lobbying culminated in the publication, in all main languages, of a long interview with Ratzinger himself, in book form.[4] This intervention had the effect of disseminating a markedly alarmist and negative view of the state of the Church, in which criticism of the present state—valid on certain points, it must be said—went so far as to attack the validity of the second Vatican Council itself.

It was inevitable that Ratzinger's call for a *'recentrage'* of Christian life and a 'restoration' of tradition should have become a reference point during the lead up to the Synod, particularly in view of the lack of a responsible basis for reflection formulated by the bodies institutionally set up for the preparation of the assembly. Even the conclusions stemming from the work of the International Theological Commission were kept shrouded in virtually impenetrable mists and only made public in the last few days before the opening of the Synod, despite the fact that they dealt with the ecclesiology of Vatican II.

The unfortunate inheritors of this situation were the '*relator*' entrusted with presenting the preliminary reports to the Synod and the special secretary, *Cardinal Danneels and Professor Walter Kasper*. We know that the opening session on November 25th found itself faced with a report of somewhat modest pretensions, empirically constructed, hardly questioning, though still open to additions, developments and corrections. It is neither difficult nor arbitrary to imagine that if the episcopal conferences had been allowed to publicise their reports, and in particular to interchange them among each other, the Synod would have been able to save a good portion of the short time allotted to it, and carry out its work in a more profitable manner.

The foregoing observations are not designed so much to criticise the preparations for the Extraordinary Synod as to draw attention to the fact that these preparations, with their undoubted anomalies, produced *interesting results on the way the assembly developed*, and—above all—favoured the appearance of a significant ecclesial grouping that would otherwise have been difficult to see emerging. There are good reasons for asking whether the 1985 Synod did not produce a *real change in the short history of this particular institution of the Catholic Church*, shown in the unprecedented fact of synodal conclusions in the true sense, that is submitted to the vote of the assembly and exempt from being reworked by the Holy See. What seems even more interesting to me, however, is an attempted evaluation of this synodal experience from a broader and more complex viewpoint, as would be suggested by the breadth and complexity of the synodal agenda itself: the *reception of Vatican II by the Church*.

A comparison, however summary, between the way the *Council developed and the way the Synod did*, reveals major differences, by no means marginal or lacking in significance. In the first place, it is noticeable that while the preparatory material for Vatican II—that is, the suggestions sent in by the bishops during the consultations of 1959–60—turned out to be far poorer and more reactionary than the conciliar debates and the conclusions that came out of them, *in 1985 the frontiers were represented by the preliminary reports from the bishops' conferences*, compared to which the synodal conclusions in their various phases appeared timorous, uncertain and even contradictory. The leadership of the Synod was undoubtedly provided by the initial reports, while the assembly itself turned out to be lacking in direction and reluctant to put forward strong and meaningful views.

This fact is linked to another, quantitative in order but still significant in its results. I refer to the numerical superiority of synodal fathers from *geographical and cultural areas other than European and North American*, a far greater and more significant majority than applied at the time of Vatican II.[5] The spread of Catholicism over the whole planet was far more in evidence here than at any of the preceding synods. This is a process that has been going on for decades, but received an enormous impetus and acceleration from the Council itself.

In the years of the Council, 1962–5, the bishops from the 'periphery' had formed a sort of outer circle in the conciliar assemblies, more liable to be led than to lead, while the bishops from central Europe played the part of protagonists of renewal, which had been undergoing a long and fruitful period of preparation and trial in their churches.[6] In the 1985 Synod this situation had changed to a spectacular extent, in that it was the churches of Latin America, Africa, Asia and Eastern Europe that, through their bishops, played the more dynamic part, produced the richest and freshest contributions and pointed out the lines most conducive to further development.

The structures and the conclusions of the Synod were both slow in adjusting to this new situation, but this is a *recurrent aspect of the relationship between historical dynamism and institutions.* It still provides a good opportunity for asking what the causes and effects of such changes might be and what prospects they open up for the life of the Catholic Church in the imminent passage into the new millenium. Here there is a danger of falling back on incidental explanations that can be distracting.

The *hegemony, though still embryonic, of non European or North American churches,* can easily be seen to stem from the intense political and ideological, but also economic and technological, evolution of the various continental or sub-continental areas. But such observations would be inadequate if they were not correlated with the *influence of Vatican II* over the past two decades, particularly in promoting self-realisation and responsibility, even though its influence in these respects was at first resisted, or at least misunderstood. The most obvious proof of Vatican II's influence is provided by the inverse ratio of influence of the 'third World' countries in the world at large and in the Church. On the political level, the promising spring of the sixties has been followed by a static period and even a decline; on the ecclesial level on the other hand—particularly as far as the Catholic Church is concerned—there has been an uninterrupted process of growth in importance leading to the threshold of hegemony.

Together with this aspect, the 1985 Synod produced evidence of the growing differentiation between the ways these churches see themselves and act, and the usual style of the European and North American churches. And it is becoming increasingly clear that the *growing cultural and social importance of these newly evangelised or recently autonomous churches* does not come from a transposition of existing models, but is based above all on their capacity to insert themselves in the Christian tradition in a creative fashion through a dynamic symbiosis with their respective cultures, just as Vatican II suggested and encouraged them to do. One gets the impression that the 1985 Synod acted as a detonator of the potentialities implicit in such situations, showing the effects that can be achieved in at least some of them.

To gain a better understanding of the new situation brought to light at the Synod, let us briefly look at the image of Vatican II which emerged from the reports by the bishops' conferences and the Synod discussions. The first impression is that a *fragmentary and almost episodic view of the Council as a collection of documents prevailed,* with greater attention being paid to the

Constitutions (*Sacrosanctum Concilium, Dei Verbum, Lumen Gentium, Gaudium et Spes*), though even these were taken in isolation, one after the other. One needs to bear in mind that this was in accordance with the approach taken in the first years after the Council, and with the suggestions contained in the letter-questionnaire sent out by Mgr Tomko.

A deeper analysis, particularly of the replies sent by the conferences, reveals a world-wide appreciation of the Council as an event that, after twenty years, can begin to be seen as historical, while at the same time signifying something richer and fuller than the sum total of its documents. What emerges is a tendency to *assimilate Vatican II as a call from the Spirit to the churches*, summoning them to a more conscious faith and an ever-renewed evangelical endeavour.[7]

There are at least *three points* that show this openness to an overall view of the Council with particular clarity. The first is the acquiring of a *truly universal understanding* in which to set the problems of Christian witness. The younger churches have shown that they are more and more adopting such a viewpoint, serenely—that is without polemic, but also without regrets— abandoning the age-old Euro-centric attitude that was still so much in evidence at Vatican II. What is important to realise here is that this marks the end not only of the reduction of Catholicism to its European-North American axis, but also of the tenacious hegemony which this has exercised over the areas of 'new' Catholicism. Vatican II marks the end of the mono-centrism of the Catholic Church and the emergence of a *poly-centrism* analogous— though with marked differences—to that of the churches of the first centuries.

A second important aspect of this process of reception of Vatican II deals with the *binomial evangelisation-enculturation*, in the sense of the Church realising that its condition is not one of 'stability' but of continuing change. This implies the centrality of missionary effort in proclaiming the Gospel and proclaiming it in poverty, that is in a way that does not—and does not seek to—trust in social privileges and 'exemptions'. A proclamation furthermore, that knows it cannot be authentic outside a real meeting with humanity and human cultural inheritances, so rich in their own values and also in traces of the Gospel. This understanding inevitably steers the Church toward a *radical revision of the concept of tradition* as it has been formed and developed in an increasingly mono-cultural setting. The comment of many conferences that Vatican II coincided with the dawning of their own churches was not merely a historical observation!

The third point is the emergence of a *capacity to appreciate the dynamism of history* and an effort to understand its connections with the life of the Church. This is a new factor in Catholicism and 'Christendom', particularly that of the post-Tridentine period, which was dominated by the claims of an a-temporal, and finally supra-temporal, view of the Christian condition, leading eventually to the opposition of sacred history to profane history. By the time we reach this twentieth anniversary of Vatican II, it has been generally accepted that Christians and their communities not only live in history, but in deep solidarity with the experiences of human society, involved in reading and proclaiming the 'signs of the times'.[8]

To the extent that such an analysis is correct, *the possibilities opened up by the Extraordinary Synod look much more significant and positive than the impression given by its final documents.*[9] Looking beyond these, one can see the 1985 Synod as mainly a process of taking stock of a continuing evolution—founded on Vatican II but with other contributory factors—going on at the heart of the Catholic Church. The Synod served as a sort of echochamber of this evolution; it declined to attempt to formulate it and thereby avoided the risk of numbing it, suffocating its dynamism and restraining its creativity. One might well ask if such a prudent approach is not an interesting symptom of a transition in the way the Petrine office's service of unity is exercised.

It might be useful to try to *sum up*, even if only provisionally, the *salient aspects of the evolution* of the Church that emerged from the Synod. The first observation to make is that this evolution is taking place above all on the *pastoral level*, in the complex sense given to this term by John XXIII and subsequently as the central and aggregating nucleus of Catholic life, to which all its other aspects—theological, spiritual, disciplinary, moral—need to be related.[10] It is precisely on the pastoral level that the pre-synod reports from the bishops' conferences point to a *variegated multiplicity of ecclesial experiences* going beyond any uniform schematisation and putting Catholic unity at risk in a way that has not happened for centuries.

That is to say that what we are witnessing now is the churches 'being' in a way that is not the result of more or less faithful and coherent application of *one* particular ecclesiogical model, but is rather the response of faith, guided by the promptings of the Spirit, to the enquiries, problems and challenges posed by different cultures and their particular circumstances to Christian communities. What is emerging strongly is a conscious acceptance of the variety of fruitful legitimacy of each community, as of their limits and the vital need for a *symphonic integration in communion.*[11] This is a clear sign that *ecclesiology itself is becoming obsolete*, which is something much more important than the passing of a single ecclesiological model. It seems to me that what has been brought to crisis-point is the very plausibility of ecclesiology as an autonomous discipline and therefore the plausibility of thinking about the Church apart from the main headings of all reflection on Christianity.

Many people observed that Vatican II brought about a Copernican revolution in the Church's self-understanding, abandoning the universalist viewpoint (which in fact had always been a 'regional' viewpoint, co-extensive with Western culture, that is) in favour of a 'local' viewpoint. But it is precisely this change that has brought the basic conditioning of ecclesiology into the limelight, showing it to be incapable of rising to an effectively multicultural situation, such as has developed in post-conciliar Catholicism. It is not irrelevant that ecclesiology as an autonomous discipline was born in the eleventh and twelfth centuries, when Western Christianity was becoming ever more mono-cultural, and prospered in direct proportion to the progressive symbiosis of Catholicism with a single culture. And it should be added that the *end of ecclesiology* has another concomitant cause in the slackening of confrontation—often tinged with competitiveness—between Church and State, helped on by the advanced process of shift in modern conditions from 'national' holding of political power to its detention by multi-national groupings and dominant economic interests.

The varied proliferation of ecclesial experiences as a result of Vatican II seems, then, to point to a definitive turn toward a *more directly evangelical inspiration behind the life of the Church*, with an abandonment of the political theory and social philosophy that conditioned the conception of the Church dominant over the past few centuries, eventually producing their formalisation in an autonomous discipline. So classical schemes such as the vertical or pyramidal approach, or the horizontalist view, used to denote the structure of the Church, seem destined for rapid obsolescence. The result of this is a necessary re-examination of images such as 'vertices', 'centre' and 'periphery', while the ministries of the different churches have become ever more mobile, not excluding the church of Rome and its bishop: several conferences remarked on the dynamic impact made by papal journeys.[12]

In the outlook briefly sketched here, the Gospel—and therefore the Incarnation, the Cross, the Resurrection, the Trinity, *koinonia*, the poor and hope of the Kingdom—will be able fully to recover its role as nucleus and unifying norm of the nature of the Church and its life,[13] while the experiences and structures of the People of God on their way[14] will take on characteristics of variability and instrumentality. To take up an old distinction, the *status ecclesiae*, that is, Christ and faith in him, will form the common and permanent element of the Church, while the *statuta ecclesiae*, that is all that concerns the life of the community, will be the place for pluriformity.[15] This will result in the pulverisation of any sort of legal processes of an ecclesiological nature and open up the possibility of an ever deeper reintegration of the Church and its reflection on its life in the realm of faith.[16] In so far as this prospect affirms and consolidates the aims of Vatican II and of John XXIII in convoking it, it takes on all the weight of a creative return to the 'great tradition' that presided over that moment of grace in now distant 1959.

Translated by Paul Burns

Notes

1. *Synode extraordinaire. Célébration de Vatican II* Intr. by J.A. Komonchak (Paris 1986) p. 285.
2. The following members of the permanent secretariat (elected after the 1983 Synod) did not take part in the Synod: Cardinal Arns, Archbishop of Sao Paulo; Cardinal Sin, Archbishop of Manila; Archbishop López Trujillo of Medellín; Archbishop Martini of Milan.
3. In view of the importance of these reports, as forming a direct source of information on the state of the Church in the mid-eighties, this article is based mainly on them, while not ignoring other sources relevant to the work of the Synod.
4. *Rapporto sulla fede*, interview by V. Messori (Rome 1985). Among the many responses to this 'report', those collected in *New Blackfriars* 66 (1985), pp. 259–308, entitled 'Special Issue. Ratzinger on the Faith: a British theological Response', are of special interest, as is J.L. Segundo *Theology and the Church. A response to Cardinal Ratzinger and a Warning to the whole Church* (Washington 1985).
5. This change is reflected too in the composition of the presidents appointed, of whom only one was European, another North American and another African. Remember that of the four Moderators at Vatican II three were European, while the other was Asiatic in origin but held a curial post. In view of this it seemed disappointing that two Europeans (though both eminently worthy) should be appointed as Relator and Special Secretary.
6. See R. Caporale *Les Hommes du Concile. Etude sociologique sur Vatican II* (Paris 1965); see also the article by Jan Kerkhofs in this issue.
7. On this point, see my essay 'La condizione cristiana dopo il Vatican II' in *Il Vaticano II e la chiesa* ed. G. Alberigo & J.J. Jossua (Brescia 1985) pp. 9–40.
8. In the period following the Council of Trent and even more after the French Revolution and the end of the *ancien régime*, Catholicism became imbued not only with a predominantly defensive attitude but with a growing mistrust in its dealings with secular history, which it saw as dominated by demonic forces inimical to faith and the Church. This conviction found institutional expression in the centralisation in the papacy of decisions concerning relations with secular cultures, from the Chinese Rites question and that of Reductions in Latin America up to the recent agreements through concordats. As early as the 1580's, Charles Borromeo experienced Rome's jealous mistrust of his initiatives to find a *modus vivendi* with the Spanish monarch through his understanding of the new concept of sovereignty held by Philip II. See 'Cristianesimo e Storia nel Vaticano II' in *Cristianesimo nella Storia* 5 (1974) pp 577–92.
9. It is somewhat difficult to decide what theological status the final Report has. It was drawn up in an authoritative literary style, that is, it proceeds to observe rather

than to innovate; it was voted on by the assembly, but the assembly had no opportunity to play a direct part in its composition; it was approved by the pope and therefore no longer has the character of a consultative document.

10. There were some curious reductive definitions of the word 'pastoral', among which that contained in the report of the German bishops' conference stands out for its punctiliousness. As is known, 'pastoral' is a key word expressing the way Angelo Roncalli saw the Church. In fact, he wanted to call the Council he convoked a 'pastoral Council'. 'Pastoral' and words with associated roots play a major part in his writings, occuring more than 2000 times in his writings, according to the verbal concordance produced by computer at the *Instituto per le Scienze religiose* at Bologna. See E. Klinger 'Der Glaube des Konzils. Eine dogmatischer Fortschritt' in *Glaube im Prozess. Cristsein nach dem II Vaticanum. Fur K. Rahner* ed. E. Klinger & K. Wittstadt (Freiburg) pp. 615–26.

11. The constant endeavour of almost all the conference reports to deepen and substantiate the ecclesial significance of bishops' conferences and the importance of the principle of subsidiarity should be viewed in this light.

12. From this point of view it is logical that several conferences should have once again raised the problem of the suitability of the Roman curia for serving communion among the churches. See G. Alberigo 'Serving the Communion of Churches' in *Concilium* 127 (7/1979) pp. 12–33.

13. Eastern Orthodox theology has already moved in this direction, putting forward the formula of eucharistic ecclesiology (cf N. Afanasieff *L'Eglise du Saint-Esprit*, Paris 1975). Such a formula is an effective expression of the endeavour to re-absorb ecclesiology within the sacramental and 'mysterial' vision of Christian revelation.

14. The debate on the suitability of defining the Church as 'people of God', which re-echoed through the synodal debates, the document of the International Theological Commission and the *Relation finalis* look like a rearguard action in relation either to the weight of Old Testament support for such a definition, or to the ever-increasing *sensus fidei* in its favour, as is shown, once more, by the reports from the conferences. A purely abstract discussion of the so-called sociological pollution of the notion of 'people of God' would be the equivalent of refusing the term 'body of Christ' because it left itself open to a materialistic interpretation!

15. The rich and robust Catholic tradition provides a guarantee against any temptation of a 'congregationalist' nature, which is in any case foreign to the spirit and experience of the churches of the various continents, as the reports from the conferences show.

16. No need to underline the fruitful implications that developments in this direction could have for new ecumenical progress.

Contributors

GIUSEPPE ALBERIGO was born in Varese in 1926 and lectures in history at the Faculty of Political Studies at Bologna university. He is also secretary of the Institute for Religious Studies in Bologna, editor of the quarterly Review *Christianesimo nella Storia*, and a member of the international committee of *Concilium*. His publications include books (mostly in Italian) on the Council of Trent, the development of the concept of power in the Church, Collegiality and Pope John XXII, the genesis of *Lumen Gentium*, conciliarism and the reception of Vatican II.

AVERY DULLES, SJ, born 1918, entered the Jesuit order in 1946 and was ordained to the priesthood in 1956. Since 1974 he has been a professor of theology at The Catholic University of America, Washington, D.C. A past president of the Catholic Theological Society of America (1975-76) and of the American Theological Society (1978-79), he has written some fifteen books and numerous articles for theological journals. Among his recent publications are *Models of Revelation* (1983) and *The Catholicity of the Church* (1985).

JACQUES GAILLOT was born at Saint-Dizier (Haute-Marne) in 1935, was ordained priest in 1961, and completed his theological studies in Rome. After periods of teaching in the seminaries at Châlons-sur-Marne and Reims, he took charge, in 1973, of the I.F.E.C. (Training Institute for Educators of the Clergy) in Paris, and was also, until 1977, Secretary of the Episcopal Commission for the Clergy and Seminaries. He was Vicar General of Langres from 1977 until 1982, when he became Bishop of Evreux.

PETER HUIZING was born in 1911 in Haarlem in the Netherlands. He studied law at the universities of Amsterdam and Nijmegen, philosophy and theology in the faculties of the Society of Jesus at Nijmegen and Maastricht and canon law at the Catholic University of Louvain and the Gregorian University of Rome. He has taught in the Faculty of Theology at Maastricht, the Faculty of Canon Law of the Gregorian and at Louvain and the Faculties of Theology at Nijmegen and Tilburg and in the Department of Canon Law of the Catholic University of America at Washington. He has published articles in many different journals.

JAN KERKHOFS, SJ born in 1924, was ordained a priest in the Society of Jesus in 1956. He taught moral theology at Louvain and general sociology at Antwerp. From 1963 to 1981 he was secretary general of the international foundation Pro Mundi Vita. At present he is professor of pastoral theology at the Catholic University of Louvain. He is also chairman of the steering committee of the European Value Systems Study Group and, since 1966, international spiritual adviser to UNIAPAC (the international Christian employers' association). Among his works have been *De Kerk in Vlaanderen* (1982), *Morgen is er al* (1976), *De Stille Omkeer* (1984).

JOSEPH KOMONCHAK was born in Nyack, New York, in 1939, and was ordained in 1963. After serving in a parish for three years, he taught systematic theology at St. Joseph's Seminary for ten years. Since 1977 he has been associate professor of theology in the Department of Religion and Religious Education at the Catholic University of America, Washington, D.C. He has published articles in various theological journals on the *magisterium*, the local Church, modern Roman Catholicism, and the Second Vatican Council.

ALOÍSIO LORSCHEIDER OFM was born in Estrela, in the Brazilian state of Rio Grande do Sul, in 1924. He entered the Franciscan friars minor in 1942 and was ordained priest in 1948. He obtained his licenciate and doctorate in theology from the Antonianum. He was ordained bishop in 1962 and appointed to Santo Ângelo in Rio Grande do Sul. In February 1973 he was transferred to Fortaleza as metropolitan archbishop. Paul VI made him a cardinal in May 1976. He has been secretary general of the Brazilian Bishops' Conference and was its president for two terms (1971-1979). He was also president of the Latin American Episcopal Conference for three years, and co-president of the Third General Conference of the Latin American Bishops. His writings consist mainly of articles and short studies of Vatican II, Puebla and theology for preaching and life.

BERARD MARTHALER, OFMConv., holds doctorates in theology

(Rome) and history (University of Minnesota). He is Professor of Religion and Religious Education at the Catholic University of America, Washington, D.C. where he has been a member of the faculty since 1963. Father Marthaler is executive editor of *The Living Light*, an interdisciplinary review of Catholic religious education, catechesis and pastoral ministry, published under the auspices of the United States Catholic Conference.

ALBERTO MELLONI was born in 1959 at Reggio Emilia. He studied history in the University of Bologna first with A. Roveri, then with D. Menozzi. From 1981 he worked with G. Alberigo on research on John XXIII in the Institute of Religious Sciences at Bologna, of which he is a member. He has published various essays on Roncalli sources and on the pope's writings, for which he has compiled a concordance. In 1985 he studied medieval canon law with B. Tierney at Cornell University of Ithaca NY within the framework of a research project set up by the Bologna Institute on the forms of Christendom.

RONALDO MUÑOZ was born in Santiago de Chile in 1933. After joining the Picpus Fathers, he studied theology and philosophy in Chile and was ordained priest. He gained a licenciate in theology from the Gregorian University and a doctorate from the Institut Catholique in Paris. Since 1964 he has taught theology and been a member of various theological commissions at Chilean and Latin American levels. Since 1972 he has been curate in a working-class district of Santiago and since 1982 has been editor of the journal *Pastoral Popular*. His most recent publication is *La Iglesia en el Pueblo: hacia una ecclesiología latinoamericana* (1984).

HERMANN POTTMEYER is Professor of Fundamental Theology at the Faculty of Catholic Theology of the University of Bochum. His publications include *Der Glaube vor dem Anspruch der Wissenschaft* (1968); *Unfehlbarkeit und Souveränität* (1975). He is co-editor of a number of works: G. Alberigo/Y. Congar/H. J. Pottmeyer *Kirche im Wandel* (1982); W. Kern/H. J. Pottmeyer/M. Seckler *Handbuch der Fundamentaltheologie* 4 vols (1985-86); H.J. Pottmeyer/G. Alberigo/J.-P. Jossua *Die Rezeption des Zweiten Vatikanischen Konzils* (1986).

JAMES PROVOST was born in Washington, DC in 1939. After theological studies at the University of Louvain, Belgium, he was ordained in 1963 for the diocese of Helena, Montana. He obtained a doctorate in canon law (JCD) at the Lateran University, Rome, in 1967, and from 1967 to 1979 served as chancellor and officialis for the diocese of Helena. In 1979 he joined the faculty of canon law at The Catholic University of America; he also became managing editor of *The Jurist* at that time. Since 1980 he has additionally served as executive coordinator of the Canon Law Society of America.

GIUSEPPE RUGGIERI teaches fundamental theology at the Theological Studium of St Paul in Catania. He is a member of the editorial board of the Bologna Review *Cristianesimo nella Storia* and of the board of Editorial Directors of *Concilium*. His published works include *La Compagnia della fede. Linee di teologia fondamentale* (1980) and (with I. Mancini) *Fede e cultura* (1979).

HENRI TEISSIER was born at Lyons in 1929. After studying philology at Rabat and philosophy at the Sorbonne, he read theology at the Paris Catholic Institute (1949-55). He obtained his diploma in Arabic from the department of oriental languages then specialised in Islamic sciences at the Dominican Institute of oriental studies and at Cairo University (1956-58). As a priest of the diocese of Algiers he took Algerian nationality and carried out the duties of secretary general of works, then those of director of the Centre of Languages and Pastoral Work. He was ordained Bishop of Oran in 1973 and returned to Algiers as Cardinal Duval's coadjutor archbishop in 1981. He is vice-president of Caritas Internationalis (since 1979), chairman of the North African episcopal conference (since 1982), and a member of the Synod secretariat council (since 1983), and has published several articles on Islamic-Christian dialogue and the theology of mission, and two books: *Eglise en Islam* (1984) and *La Mission de l'Eglise* (1985).

JEAN-MARIE TILLARD OP was born in St Pierre and Miquelon (French overseas territory). He became a Dominican in 1950. He studied at Rome (philosophy) and Le Saulchoir (Paris). He was a *peritus* at Vatican II. Since then, in addition to a teaching post in the Ottawa Dominican faculty, he has been busily committed to matters ecumenical: Anglican-Catholic commission (ARCIC), Orthodox-Catholic commission, Faith and Order (Vice-chairman). He has written works of ecumenical import: *L'Eucharistie Pâque de l'Eglise* (1984), *Devant Dieu et pour le monde: le projet des réligieux* (1974), *Il y a charisme et charisme* (1977), *L'éveque de Rome* (1982). He contributes to *Irénikon, Lumen Vitae, Nouvelle Revue Théologique, Proche-Orient chrétien, One in Christ,* and *Midway.*

ELIAS ZOGHBY was born in Cairo in 1912, ordained in 1936 and served in Palestine, Egypt and the Sudan before being consecrated Greek Catholic Archbishop of Baalbeck (Lebanon) in 1968. His publications include: a commentary on Saint Matthew; a study of the Lebanon; *All Schismatics* (also published in English) and numerous articles on ecumenical subjects in French-language journals.

CONCILIUM

CONCILIUM

CONCILIUM 1985

All back issues are still in print: available from bookshops (price £3.95) or direct from the publisher (£4.45/US$7.70/Can$8.70 including postage and packing).

T. & T. CLARK LTD, 59 GEORGE STREET, EDINBURGH EH2 2LQ, SCOTLAND